SEP 5

ACT II, SC 5   ACT I, SC 5
        SC 4   SC 2
        SC 3

Photo by Jim Ball

A scene from the Bathhouse Theatre production of "Sherlock's Veiled Secret."

SHERLOCK'S VEILED SECRET

BY K.C. BROWN

Based on a story by
K.C. Brown and Arne Zaslove

DRAMATISTS
PLAY SERVICE
INC.

SHERLOCK'S VEILED SECRET was produced by The Bathhouse Theatre (Arne Zaslove, Artistic Director; Phil Peters, Managing Director), in Seattle, Washington, on May 3, 1994. It was directed by Daniel Wilson; the set design was by Greg Elder; the costume design was by Carl S. Bronsdon; the lighting design was by Judy Wolcott; the sound design was by Eric Chappelle and the stage manager was Jeannie Wood-Elder. The cast was as follows:

VIOLET SHERIDAN .... Kymberli Colbourne
SHERLOCK HOLMES .... Terry Edward Moore
CHARLES WELLINGTON YORKE .... William Hamer
MRS. CYRIL MORTON .... Teresa Castracane
IRENE ADLER .... Ellen Boyle
TURLOUGH O'BRENNAN .... Timothy Hyland
LADY CHARLOTTE
          CARRINGTON .... Margaret VandenBerghe

CHARACTERS
(in order of appearance)

VIOLET SHERIDAN — 20s, sculptor. Intelligent and strong-willed.

SHERLOCK HOLMES — Aged 66, in retirement.

CHARLES WELLINGTON YORKE — Late 20s, from an upper class family. Boyish, energetic, charming — but not free from the constraints of his background.

MRS. CYRIL MORTON nee VIOLET SMITH — In her 40s, poised. A woman of deep feeling and some wealth. Appears in flashback as a woman in her 20s.

IRENE ADLER — Opera singer, actress, adventuress, now in her early 60's. Appears in flashback as a woman of 30.

TURLOUGH O'BRENNAN — 30s–mid-40s. Flamboyant, possessed of a convincing charm and a good sense of humour.

LADY CHARLOTTE CARRINGTON — Mid-40s or so. Married to a peer of the realm. Upper crust sangfroid concealing passion and an adventurous spirit.

SHERLOCK'S VEILED SECRET

ACT ONE

Scene 1

Sussex, England; a country garden: roses and hollyhocks. The year is 1920. Loud buzzing is heard, as of swarms of bees. A man sits dozing in a garden chair next to a table strewn with papers. It is Sherlock Holmes, aged about 66. His sleep is restless. The light changes, as if a cloud passed over the sun. The sound of bees distorts into something strange and menacing. We hear voices, possibly distorted.

SHERLOCK. *(Voice over.)* Are you sure?
WOMAN. *(Voice over.)* There's no question. Blackmail.
SHERLOCK. *(Voice over.)* Damn!
WOMAN. *(Voice over.)* You've got to help me.
SHERLOCK. *(Voice over.)* I'll lay plans in my own way.
WOMAN. *(Voice over.)* But hurry.
SHERLOCK. *(Voice over.)* It may take time.
WOMAN. *(Voice over.)* No question. Blackmail.
SHERLOCK. *(Voice over.)* In my own way ...
WOMAN. *(Voice over.)* You've got to help me. *(Sherlock suddenly shakes himself awake. The lighting changes, the bees once again sound like bees. Something in the landscape has changed, though. A young woman stands on the garden path, watching him. The young woman is in her early twenties, well dressed, with a somewhat bohemian flair.)*
VIOLET. Mr. Holmes?
SHERLOCK. *(Still disoriented.)* I beg your pardon?
VIOLET. I'm Violet Sheridan. You invited me — that is, you asked me to come.

SHERLOCK. Oh — yes. Oh, yes, forgive me. *(Sherlock looks long and hard at her. Violet is shy and uncomfortable, left standing under the scrutiny of this legendary figure. At long last he breaks the silence, although he does not yet invite her to sit down. From time to time in what follows he pauses to stare at her, adding to Violet's discomfort.)* I'm sorry you found no cabs available at the train station.

VIOLET. Oh. I do hope my tardiness has not inconvenienced you.

SHERLOCK. It is of no consequence, I assure you. I am glad you were able to catch a lift from the edge of town, at least.

VIOLET. *(Surprised.)* Yes. How did you — ? You must have many visitors, Mr. Holmes.

SHERLOCK. On the contrary.

VIOLET. Yet you are familiar not only with the train schedule but with the time it takes to reach here from the station by various means ...

SHERLOCK. Retirement does not incline one to pay such close attention to the time, Miss Sheridan. No, it is simply that the road here from the edge of town is unpaved. Had you walked all the way your boots would be dusty, but in fact they show only a small trace of loam around the sole — the kind of loose but exceptionally fertile soil which characterizes not only my pathway but, I might add, my entire property. It stands out among the acreages here, if I may say so. Also, there is a cab stand at the edge of town beside which is a large clump of lilies. You evidently stopped there and turned to see whether any cabs approached. Your left sleeve brushed the lilies as you turned to look. Observe where they have left their tell-tale smear of pollen.

VIOLET. Oh. I see.

SHERLOCK. *(Not unkindly.)* Very difficult to launder, I should point out. *(Their eyes meet, at this evident reference to Miss Sheridan's evidently slightly impecunious state.)*

VIOLET. *(After a pause.)* Mr. Holmes, you've yet to tell me why I was summoned here.

SHERLOCK. Would you care for some tea, Miss Sheridan? I believe my housekeeper has laid out a tray.

6

VIOLET. Thank you.

SHERLOCK. I won't be a moment. Pray, excuse me. *(Violet is somewhat relieved to have a breather. She drifts over to the table. At first she restrains herself from looking through the papers which are strewn over it. But since Holmes is gone a long time, she eventually finds she cannot resist. Very surreptitiously, she lifts a paper or two. Holmes reappears suddenly and Violet has to drop them suddenly.)*

VIOLET. May I clear for you? *(But he has deposited the tea tray smack on top of the papers before she can move to tidy up. He pours, somewhat carelessly, and passes her a teacup but takes none for himself. Violet is obliged to reach for her cream and sugar. He has fallen into a reverie.)* I was admiring your setting here, Mr. Holmes.

SHERLOCK. Ahh, yes.

VIOLET. I see you keep bees.

SHERLOCK. Mm.

> "I will arise now and go, and go to Innisfree,
> And a small cabin build there, of clay and wattles
>   made: – "

VIOLET.

> "Nine bean rows will I have there, a hive for the
>   honey-bee,
> And live alone in the bee-loud glade."

SHERLOCK. *(With satisfaction.)* I see you know your Irish poets, Miss Sheridan.

VIOLET. I was fortunate to receive a very good education. *(Pause.)*

SHERLOCK. Good.

> "And I shall have some peace there, for peace comes
>   dropping slow,
> Dropping from the veils of the morning to where the
>   cricket sings;"

VIOLET. *(Joining him.)*

> "There midnight's all a glimmer, and noon a purple glow,
> And evening full of the linnet's wings."*

* Poem by William Butler Yeats.

7

(Pause.) Do you find it peaceful here, Mr. Holmes?

SHERLOCK.   Wretchedly. Miss Sheridan, perhaps we should proceed to business. So you are not aware of why I have summoned you.

VIOLET.   I must say, Mr. Holmes, that I am quite in the dark. To have the opportunity to meet a man of such eminence — *(He waves away whatever she is about to say with his hand.)*

SHERLOCK.   Then you have no idea.

VIOLET.   I did dare to flatter myself ...

SHERLOCK.   How so?

VIOLET.   I suppose you know that I am a sculptor. I mean, I suppose that is how I came to your attention. I dared to think that perhaps you might wish, in retirement, for a bust to be done. *(Holmes laughs suddenly, derisively, rudely.)*

SHERLOCK.   Nonsense, Miss Sheridan. I am currently at work on a case.... Yes, even in retirement an exceptional case will sometimes seek me out. It is important that I ascertain whether you are the person I believe you to be.

VIOLET.   In connection with a case? I don't understand. I know of no —

SHERLOCK.   Quite right. You know of no connection you might have. Allow me to ask you a few questions. If I may.

VIOLET.   *(Uncertain.)* Certainly.

SHERLOCK.   You are currently showing some of your work in a prominent London gallery.

VIOLET.   Yes. I have the good fortune —

SHERLOCK.   It is good fortune for one so young, but no doubt your talent justifies your success. Are you one of the distinguished Sheridans of literary fame?

VIOLET.   *(Dropping her head.)* I do not know.

SHERLOCK.   Indeed?

VIOLET.   The named was bestowed upon me.

SHERLOCK.   Bestowed.

VIOLET.   By a headmistress with literary pretensions.

SHERLOCK.   Ahh. In an Irish school?

VIOLET.   No. *(Pause.)*

SHERLOCK.   The notices on your gallery show mention that your work has a freshness and originality.

VIOLET.   Thank you.

SHERLOCK.   From which I take it that you did not study in England.

VIOLET.   That is true. I was raised — or rather, grew up on the Continent.

SHERLOCK.   Paris?

VIOLET.   Switzerland.

SHERLOCK.   I was not aware of any great art academies in Switzerland.

VIOLET.   Such training as I have I acquired at the boarding school I attended.

SHERLOCK.   Run by a headmistress with literary pretensions.

VIOLET.   Yes.

SHERLOCK.   With a penchant for bestowing last names.

VIOLET.   *(Hesitating.)* Quite.

SHERLOCK.   But only, presumably, upon those students who were in need of one. *(Violet is silent.)* There's no shame in wearing a name with such a fine pedigree. I presume you were born in England?

VIOLET.   I presume so.

SHERLOCK.   You have only a presumption on the matter?

VIOLET.   Yes. That is to say, I have no documents. *(Sherlock waits.)* They were not delivered with me. They probably went missing — or were destroyed.

SHERLOCK.   'Delivered' is an interesting word.

VIOLET.   It is the only one which applies.

SHERLOCK.   You were delivered at this boarding school by your parents?

VIOLET.   I believe so.

SHERLOCK.   A strange thing to be unsure of.

VIOLET.   I was an infant at the time, Mr. Holmes. There are few details I could attest to that would stand up in a court of law.

SHERLOCK.   Quite. Yet the headmistress to whom you were 'delivered' must have told you something of the circumstances...?

VIOLET.   Mr. Holmes, I don't know what conclusion you draw from my ... my lack of background. I assure you my life

9

and conduct have been respectable in every regard.

SHERLOCK.   I draw no conclusion. I am merely assembling the facts. Pray, continue.

VIOLET.   Continue?

SHERLOCK.   Your 'delivery' at this boarding school ... *(Sherlock waits. Finally Violet goes on.)*

VIOLET.   The headmistress was left with strict instructions never to reveal my origins to me. The lady who brought me, she says, was veiled. And the gentleman's features were barely distinguishable under a huge beard, a great handlebar moustache, and glasses. But both were said to be very well dressed and well spoken. And throughout my time there they provided for me (at least, someone did) most generously. At first I was lodged in the headmistress's own home with a nursemaid, until I was old enough to attend school. At regular intervals an anonymous bank draft would appear in the headmistress' office, earmarked for my care. You will appreciate, Mr. Holmes, that the girls with whom I attended school were all from prominent families. And I may say that my anonymous stipend was sufficient to allow me to hold up my head among them in all things.

SHERLOCK.   This headmistress, Mademoiselle — ?

VIOLET.   Le Blanc. How did you know she was French?

SHERLOCK.   She treated you ... respectfully?

VIOLET.   With utmost respect. I may even say, with some tenderness of feeling.

SHERLOCK.   Ahh.

VIOLET.   It was the only home I ever knew.

SHERLOCK.   Of course. Pray, continue.

VIOLET.   We studied languages, the natural sciences, history, philosophy — yes, drawing and sculpting (I note your bemused look, Mr. Holmes). I had the impression sometimes that someone was watching over my welfare. Watching from the shadows, as it were.

SHERLOCK.   An absurd fancy, I should think.

VIOLET.   Nevertheless. As I approached the end of my studies, I kept expecting that my mysterious benefactor (if it was not my parents, or one of them) would be revealed. I imagined there was something exotic about them that inclined them to discretion while giving me such a respectable upbringing and education. Perhaps they were world travellers. Or artists — I always wondered where my talents came from. And somehow I imagined they would step forward to claim me as I was ready to enter the world, and then we would go off together on a series of adventures. Finally I would know who I was, my life would make sense to me and would open up to wonderful romantic vistas, waiting to be explored. *(A brief silence.)*

SHERLOCK. Was it disappointing that no one claimed you?

VIOLET. *(Hiding her feelings as best she can.)* Oh, well. I had gotten accustomed to trailing veils of mystery with me. It made me somewhat popular with the other girls. And it opened up the possibility of pursuing an unconventional career. *(Pause.)* What made you think no one claimed me?

SHERLOCK. You spent the years of the Great War on the Continent?

VIOLET. I had little choice, Mr. Holmes.

SHERLOCK. Communication between England and the Continent was next to impossible ...

VIOLET. You mean, had my parents wished to contact me they might have been unable to. I suppose you are right.

SHERLOCK. So you made your way to London after the war and have enjoyed, I must say, some considerable success as an artist. Surely this success you have won on your personal merit is far more satisfying than finding your identity as someone's daughter.

VIOLET. One still has need of one's parents, Mr. Holmes.

SHERLOCK. Indeed?

VIOLET. Recently I have become engaged to a young man of good family.

SHERLOCK. *(Trying to conceal a reaction.)* Allow me to congratulate you. And you would like your parents with the deep pockets to reappear in time to give you a society wedding, no doubt. The better to vanish into respectability, give up your artistic ambitions, and molder away in some fashionable Mayfair home.

VIOLET.   That was not the life I envisioned for myself, Mr. Holmes, even as a married woman. But the point is moot. *(Seizing her opportunity.)* The veils of mystery surrounding my origin hold no romance for the family I am to marry into. In fact, I have just been asked, in the words of Mr. Oscar Wilde, "to make a definite effort to produce at any rate one parent, of either sex, before the season is quite over." I had hoped —

SHERLOCK.   Awkward. I can see where a couple of respectable parents would come in handy.

VIOLET.   Mr. Holmes, I did not wish, in quoting Mr. Wilde, to encourage you to be flippant. My marital prospects aside, this confusion about my identity has caused me all my life a deep and abiding pain.

SHERLOCK.   Please accept my apology, Miss Sheridan.

VIOLET.   In addition to which, the mystery of my identity seems to have made me, God knows how, a suspect in a case you are investigating.

SHERLOCK.   Not a suspect, exactly, Miss Sheridan. But a principal.

VIOLET.   Please — you must tell me the nature of this case. What is the crime?

SHERLOCK.   Blackmail.

VIOLET.   And how am I involved?

SHERLOCK.   I hope as a collaborator, Miss Sheridan.

VIOLET.   *(Shocked.)* What?

SHERLOCK.   I want you to work with me.

VIOLET.   I don't understand.

SHERLOCK.   It has long seemed to me that artists share some of the qualities that are crucial to the practice of my work. Their powers of observation. Their ability to fashion details into a coherent picture of reality. Observation is part of my science.... Yes, I call it a science, Miss Sheridan, although you raise your eyebrows. This treatise of mine which so intrigued you — no, I assure you, I have no objection ... curiosity is also part of my science.... This treatise of mine details the marriage of observation and deduction, for the purpose of solving crime. An artist who was rigorously trained in logic might make an admirable detective, and thereby use her powers for a socially useful purpose.

VIOLET.   *(Surprised and bemused.)* Is it your intention to recruit detectives from the ranks of the art world?

SHERLOCK.   *(Coolly.)* I should have realized that speaking of matters that are close to one's heart is not best attempted with a stranger.

VIOLET.   Please — forgive me.

SHERLOCK.   *(Musingly.)* My mother was related to the French painter, Vernet.

VIOLET.   An admirable connection, to explain your interest in art. But now I am truly mystified. Why, of all the striving artists in the world, should I have come to your attention?

SHERLOCK.   You came to my attention long before you showed any artistic inclination. You see ... I am your father, Miss Sheridan. Violet. *(For a long time, Violet cannot speak. Finally Holmes decides to help.)* No doubt you want to know who your mother is. *(Violet is barely able to nod.)* Ahh. But that I must not tell you.

Scene 2

London. Early afternoon. A spacious artist's studio, sparsely furnished. In the background we see a day-bed; perhaps this place is where Violet lodges as well as works. Violet herself has fallen asleep over a book.

Her sleep is fitful. Perhaps the lighting, again, is strange. And perhaps we actually see Sherlock in huddled conference with a veiled lady. Or perhaps we don't. We hear in voice over:

WOMAN.   *(Voice over.)* Are we decided, then?

SHERLOCK.   *(Voice over.)* I see no alternative. Do you?

WOMAN.   *(Voice over.)* Surely ...

SHERLOCK. *(Voice over.)* We've been through this, over and over.

WOMAN. *(Voice over.)* I only wish —

SHERLOCK. *(Voice over.)* We can't indulge in wishes. We must live in reality.

WOMAN. *(Voice over.)* Let's be quick then. *(The sound of a baby crying slowly transmutes into ... from offstage we hear a bell ringing [or a horn sounding — it should be an unorthodox sound]... two short rings [or toots] then a long one. Footsteps.)*

CHARLES. *(From offstage.)* Violet! I say, Violet! *(Charles Wellington Yorke enters. He is a young man and fashionably, although conservatively, dressed. Everything in his manner suggests governesses and public school. He is not, when all is said and done, devoid of humour or charm. He carries a bouquet of flowers. During the early moments of the scene he locates a silver vase — a gift of his to Violet — and proudly deposits the bouquet in it.)* Ah, there you are!

VIOLET. *(Stirring.)* Hmm?

CHARLES. Bit late for a lie-in.

VIOLET. Sorry, darling. *(Finding her place.)* Let me just finish this, would you? Help yourself. *(A tea tray is set, complete with cakes and toast. Everything is presented with bohemian aesthetic flair. Charles hurls himself at the offered goodies.)*

CHARLES. You *are* a tease — when you know I'm dying to hear about your visit. *(No answer.)* What did the great man say? Did you get a chance to ask him about your mystery? Did he take an interest? This tea is bloody awful, excuse my French. You seem to have made it with cold water. *(Still no answer. Charles starts in on the pile of tea-cakes. They evidently are not of the highest quality either, but he musters his courage manfully and manages to consume quite a few of them.)*

VIOLET. *(Under her breath.)* No, it *can't* be her.

CHARLES. Violet, darling, I really must insist —

VIOLET. What's that, Charles?

CHARLES. I'm positively bursting with curiosity. And this tea is far too dreadful to keep anyone occupied for long. I rang you up last night but there was no answer. Did Mr. Holmes keep you till all hours? Didn't he let you get home at a respectable time? I trust his behaviour was honourable.

VIOLET.   Nonsense, Charles. The hour was perfectly respectable. *(Pause.)* I went out for a walk in the evening, that's all.

CHARLES.   Well, you know I wouldn't trust any man in the face of such beauty and charm. In fact, I don't think I'll let you out alone when — Well, when you're mine.

VIOLET.   Mmm.

CHARLES.   Violet, you've got to stop! It's maddening. All you do is "Hmm" at me. What did Mr. Holmes want? What business did he have with you? How did he come to know of you? It's all very thrilling.

VIOLET.   I hope you'll find it thrilling when I explain, Charles. *(She holds up the book she's reading.)*

CHARLES.   *Adventures of Sherlock Holmes.* Ah, Dr. Watson's account. You should have boned up *before* your interview rather than after.

VIOLET.   You're right about that. I just got it from a circulating library this morning and haven't stopped reading since.

CHARLES.   *(Jokingly.)* Looking for clues?

VIOLET.   *(Surprised.)* Yes, exactly. How did you know?

CHARLES.   Violet, don't be silly. I haven't the ghost of an idea what you're on about. Why did Mr. Sherlock Holmes summon *you?* Of all people in the world. It's frightfully mysterious.

VIOLET.   It certainly is. Well, believe it or not, he asked me to help him on a case.

CHARLES.   Extraordinary!

VIOLET.   Yes. A blackmail case. I told him I wouldn't, of course.

CHARLES.   But, Violet —

VIOLET.   Because that's not the most extraordinary thing about my visit. Charles.... Everything I've believed or imagined about myself, about my life, is utterly changed since yesterday.

CHARLES.   Gosh. Meeting someone famous can have that effect, I suppose. I imagine him having sort of a magnetic force field around him. Is that what it was like?

VIOLET.   He certainly has shifted the poles — of my identity, I mean.

CHARLES.   I don't understand. How would he do such a

thing? I mean, no offence, he doesn't know you.

VIOLET. *(Choosing her words carefully.)* He's been aware of me for some time. In fact, has ... watched over me, you might call it. The only time he lost track of me, he says, was during the war. And then I resurfaced, as he put it, with the exhibit at the gallery. That's when he decided to summon me to meet him.

CHARLES. Watched over you, you say...? Why would he do such a thing? How did he know who you are? What would cause him to — ?

VIOLET. He is my father, Charles. *(A long, thunderstruck silence.)*

CHARLES. I say.

VIOLET. Indeed.

CHARLES. Well.

VIOLET. Well.

CHARLES. Sherlock Holmes — your father! It's a bit hard to believe.

VIOLET. He knew things about me that no one else could. There's no doubt, Charles. Well.... Do you think he would do? I mean, as far as your parents are concerned?

CHARLES. Well. He's not quite the retired banker we were hoping for. I suppose it would depend.... I suppose it would depend upon who your mother is.

VIOLET. Exactly.

CHARLES. And the circumstances of their ... relations.

VIOLET. Quite so.

CHARLES. Well?

VIOLET. He wouldn't tell me.

CHARLES. Wouldn't — or couldn't?

VIOLET. *Wouldn't.* I'm sure it's not nearly as tawdry as you imagine, Charles.

CHARLES. Of course, I'm sorry, darling. But ... how would one go about finding out? *(Violet holds up the book again.)* Ah, I see what you mean now. Clues.

VIOLET. There seem to be a few women he took an interest in at various times. Albeit a fleeting one.

CHARLES. And how will you determine —

VIOLET.   How will *I*? Charles, are you in this with me or are you not?

CHARLES.   Sorry, darling. Of course I am. How shall we determine which is ... your mother?

VIOLET.   We shall have to become detectives ourselves, Charles. Since the great detective himself shows no sign of offering his assistance. Or his cooperation, I might add.

CHARLES.   *(Somewhat green at the prospect.)* Oh. I see.

VIOLET.   Now, there's one here who's a clear candidate. *(Reading to him.)* "To Sherlock Holmes she is always *the* woman. I have seldom heard him mention her under any other name. In his eyes she eclipses and predominates the whole of her sex."

CHARLES.   *(Perking up.)* Oh, that *does* sound promising. What is her name? Who is she?

VIOLET.   Irene Adler. And she *was* an actress.

CHARLES.   Oh dear.

VIOLET.   Well, an opera singer.

CHARLES.   Mm. That's better, I suppose. And she is dead, is she? *(This last is said rather hopefully.)*

VIOLET.   So says Dr. Watson.

CHARLES.   Well, that's convenient, at least.

VIOLET.   Charles, how can you say such a thing? She was rather an adventuress. She had an affair with the King of Bohemia. And she married a lawyer within days of meeting Mr. Holm ... my — my father.

CHARLES.   Oh, I say. Do we have any other candidates who weren't married to someone else? Perhaps your father was *secretly* married. *(Violet picks up another volume of Watson's memoirs, this one entitled* The Return of Sherlock Holmes.*)*

VIOLET.   Well, he was secretly engaged to a chambermaid at one time.

CHARLES.   Oh, dear!

VIOLET.   But there's no further mention of her once the case was solved. Besides, it doesn't make sense. Mr. Holmes, for all his eminence, is not well-to-do. And the lady in question must have been, for look at the upbringing I received.

CHARLES.   I sincerely hope you're right.

VIOLET. And, if I may say so, my father appears in these pages as a man of rather fastidious tastes.

CHARLES. Well, that's a relief. Are there no well-bred, un-married women who figure in the accounts of his adventures?

VIOLET. He did seem rather taken, at one point, with a young lady musician.

CHARLES. Artistic talent. This is good.

VIOLET. Who had a position as a governess, but was later revealed to be heiress to a South African fortune.

CHARLES. And means! Oh, this is very promising.

VIOLET. And her name ... was Violet Smith.

CHARLES. Splendid! Oh, this all fits together. And ... un-married?

VIOLET. Well.... She was later married. To a Mr. Cyril Morton of Morton & Kennedy. Electricians. In Westminster. Apparently quite well known. And eminently respectable.

CHARLES. Yes, but ... my dear Violet. Where exactly do you figure in the story? Or, more to the point, where did Mr. Holmes?...

VIOLET. Well, that is what we must find out.

CHARLES. Quite so.

VIOLET. There is no point assuming the facts are scandal-ous when we are not in possession of them.

CHARLES. *(Heartened.)* Of course you're right. There must be a perfectly straightforward explanation. If only we can un-cover it.

VIOLET. That is what we must hope. *(Violet is already moving to gather her outdoor things. Charles rouses himself, and absent-mindedly downs a few more tea-cakes.)*

CHARLES. Where exactly do we begin?

VIOLET. Well, we must discover whether Mrs. Cyril Morton is still living.

CHARLES. And if she is?

VIOLET. We shall pay her a visit. *(Charles follows Violet, who is already on her way out the door. As a final gesture, he pauses to wash down a tea-cake with a swallow of tea, having forgotten what a mistake that could be. A grimace, and then:)*

CHARLES. Sherlock Holmes ... I say!

Scene 3

A well-appointed London parlour. From offstage we hear the sounds of a piano, expertly played. From offstage in another direction, we hear people approaching. It is the next morning.

VIOLET.　*(From offstage.)* Thank you. We'll be happy to wait. *(Violet and Charles enter, and Violet immediately begins to "case the joint.")*

CHARLES.　I say, Violet! Not so obvious, please.

VIOLET.　This may be our only chance to be alone in here. Keep an eye open for Mrs. Morton.

CHARLES.　I'll do my best, I'm sure. Now, who am I again?

VIOLET.　For goodness sake, Charles, you may be yourself if you really can't remember. But I am Miss Hunter — pray, don't forget *that.*

CHARLES.　You know, you'd look rather lovely as mistress of a parlour like this.

VIOLET.　*(Rumpling his hair affectionately.)* You great ass.

CHARLES.　Mmm. As long as I'm *your* great ass. *(Footsteps are heard from the direction where we previously heard piano music. Violet and Charles compose themselves on a sofa or a couple of chairs. Mrs. Cyril Morton appears, a well-kept lady of uncertain age. Charles rises to shake her hand.)*

MRS. MORTON.　Ahh, good morning, Mr. — *(For a brief moment, both ladies are looking at Charles, with different intent, waiting to see what will come out of his mouth.)*

CHARLES.　Umm, Thorn. Dyke.

MRS. MORTON.　Mr. Thorn ... Dyke? How nice to meet you. And you must be Miss —

VIOLET.　*(Jumping in.)* Hunter.

MRS. MORTON.　Miss Hunter. Quite. Have I kept you waiting?

CHARLES.　*(Apologetically.)* Well, we did arrive a little before our time. *(At an opportune moment, when Mrs. Morton is unable to see, Violet digs Charles firmly in the ribs.)*

MRS. MORTON.   Not at all. Now, how may I be of service to you?

VIOLET.   As I believe I mentioned to you on the telephone, Mrs. Morton, I represent a young lady who is in search of information concerning her family background. Before I begin, however, I hope you will allow me to express, on behalf of Mr. Thorn Dyke and myself, our deepest condolences on your husband's recent passing.

MRS. MORTON.   I beg your pardon?

VIOLET.   Mr. Cyril Morton. We read it in the *Times*. We are so very sorry.

CHARLES.   Very sorry.

MRS. MORTON.   No doubt you are referring to the death of my father-in-law, Mr. Cyril Morton, Senior. My husband, while not in robust health, is nevertheless, I am happy to report, very much alive. *(Violet blanches, and Charles looks as though he wished the furniture would sink through the floor.)*

VIOLET.   Oh, I am so very relieved to hear it. Allow me to offer, on behalf of Mr. Thorn Dyke and myself, our sympathy on the loss of your father-in-law.

MRS. MORTON.   *(Drily.)* Thank you.

VIOLET.   Well. To our purpose, then. My client — or rather, um, my friend — has reason to believe ... that she may have some connection with your family.

MRS. MORTON.   Indeed. Through my husband? Or, perhaps, my father-in-law?

VIOLET.   No. Well. Umm, let me begin with another line of inquiry, Mrs. Morton. Are you acquainted with Mr. Sherlock Holmes? *(Mrs. Morton is greatly taken aback. For a moment she simply stares at Violet, not knowing what to say. Pause.)*

MRS. MORTON.   *(Cautiously.)* Forgive me. I suppose your question is not so surprising after all. Many people have read Dr. Watson's account of my story. So you know that Mr. Holmes played a pivotal role in my life.

VIOLET.   Indeed. I was struck by the frank admiration Mr. Holmes evinced, according to Dr. Watson, for both your talents and your personal attributes. May I ask whether you ... stayed in touch with one another after the adventure to which you were both a party? *(Mrs. Morton lowers her head. Long pause.)*

CHARLES. *(Gently.)* Mrs. Morton, a young woman's happiness rests upon your reply.

MRS. MORTON. *(Smiling, almost bitterly.)* Does it? *(Pause.)* We did become ... friends, if I may so describe it.

VIOLET. And your Christian name, I believe, is Violet.

MRS. MORTON. It is.

VIOLET. It was some time after your first acquaintance with Mr. Holmes that you actually married Mr. Morton, was it not?

MRS. MORTON. Some time, yes. *(Charles can hardly breathe. Violet herself is on the edge of her seat.)*

VIOLET. And it was during the time of your friendship with Mr. Holmes, was it not, that he disappeared in Switzerland and was considered missing for some three years?

MRS. MORTON. No, you're quite mistaken there.

VIOLET. Am I?

MRS. MORTON. When I first met Mr. Holmes I believe he had *returned* from a lengthy sojourn abroad.

VIOLET. Ahh. Well. It is of no matter.

MRS. MORTON. Miss Hunter, you will pardon my saying so, but I should be most grateful if you would draw the thread of your inquiry back around to your friend. Or client.

VIOLET. By all means. *(Violet, however, is momentarily stumped as to how to proceed. Mrs. Morton, however, takes this opportunity to recover herself and regain control of the interview.)*

MRS. MORTON. I trust you will forgive my bluntness, Miss Hunter. My husband's business is well established and has always provided him with an upstanding position in society. It must be said, however, that when he did me the honour of making me Mrs. Morton, he married an inherited fortune beyond the scope even of his most successful ventures. Allow me to say that your "client" is not the first "long lost relative" to appear and wish to prove some family tie.

VIOLET. Mrs. Morton, to suspect my — client of mercenary motives is hardly fair. She has a genuine, a heartfelt desire to be reunited with her family, whoever they may be. *(No answer.)*

CHARLES. Perhaps we should be frank with you, Mrs. Morton. Our friend's ... connection is with Mr. Sherlock

Holmes. We had hoped you might perhaps be able to shed light on it — in view of your friendship with him. And one other detail led us to you. Our friend's name is ... Violet.

MRS. MORTON.   Miss Violet Hunter, perhaps? *(Pause.)* It's strange. You do remind me of myself when I was your age. *(Recovering herself.)* Or are you aware that one of Mr. Holmes's cases involved a Miss Violet Hunter? *(Charles and Violet exchange significant, piercing glances.)*

VIOLET.   We were not aware.

MRS. MORTON.   The case of the "Copper Beeches," I believe. You might care to look it up. If nothing else, it makes admirable reading.

VIOLET.   *(Rising.)* Mrs. Morton, I fear we have imposed upon your time too long.

MRS. MORTON.   Pray, think nothing of it. *(Charles and Violet begin their humiliating retreat. They are stopped by Mrs. Morton, whose voice is distinguished by a new and shrewder tone than we have yet heard from her.)* If you are interested in female friends of Mr. Holmes ... had you thought of looking up Miss Irene Adler?

CHARLES.   We had thought of it, Mrs. Morton. But unfortunately the lady is dead.

MRS. MORTON.   Are you quite sure?

Scene 4

The next day. We are once again in Sherlock Holmes's Sussex garden, with the sound of bees surrounding us. From offstage, we hear the sound of a violin. The table is strewn as before. The violin stops. Sherlock enters. We hear the creak of a gate, and Violet makes her way up the path.

SHERLOCK.   Ahh, Miss ... Violet. I'm glad you've arrived.

VIOLET.   You were expecting me?

SHERLOCK.   Indeed.

VIOLET.   Indeed? Why today? I'm sure the loam on my boots has nothing to reveal to you on that score.

SHERLOCK.   No, but your disappointment yesterday with Mrs. Cyril Morton suggested to me that I might be seeing you soon. *(Violet looks at him as if he were possessed by the devil.)*

VIOLET.   Now that truly is supernatural. You can have no earthly means of knowing that I paid a visit to Mrs. Morton. Much less that I came away disappointed.

SHERLOCK.   Your disappointment is hinted at in your demeanour. But really, no earthly means? Remember that when every impossible explanation is ruled out, what remains, however improbable, *must* be the truth.

VIOLET.   You are determined to instruct me in the precepts of your art.

SHERLOCK.   I am.

VIOLET.   And will you instruct me so well that I shall be able to penetrate my own mystery? *(He does not answer but looks at her deeply — looks almost into her. She looks back. Finally he speaks.)*

SHERLOCK.   I have offered to take you on as — an apprentice, if you will. Have you reconsidered?

VIOLET.   The blackmail case?

SHERLOCK.   Exactly.

VIOLET.   I thought you were in retirement.

SHERLOCK.   I could not remain in retirement when this case presented itself to me. It has implications which are more important — and more dangerous — than you can guess. *(Pause.)*

VIOLET.   You have saddled me with quite an intriguing case of my own to solve, thank you very much.

SHERLOCK.   *(With difficulty.)* It is not easy to say this but ... my health is not what it was in my first youth. Some assistance would be valuable to me.

VIOLET.   What about your friend Dr. Watson? I thought he was your favoured companion on such adventures.

SHERLOCK.   Dr. Watson is out of the country at the moment on a round-the-world cruise. A honeymoon cruise, if you please. The old bounder. I believe it's his third. Or is it his fourth?

VIOLET. *(Sharply.)* At least Dr. Watson is a believer in marriage.

SHERLOCK. *(Stung.)* You have no evidence that I am not.

VIOLET. True. You *offer* me no evidence on that point. *(Stalemate. The two adversaries regard one another, each taking the other's measure. Finally Violet, as the winner of that round, is the first to speak.)* So you wish your daughter, who has conveniently resurfaced, to fill Dr. Watson's admiring shoes.

SHERLOCK. I do not require admiration in the pursuit of my calling. It had struck me that this was an excellent opportunity to provide some education. By example, of course.

VIOLET. And what makes you think I am in need of education?

SHERLOCK. Come now, my dear. Offering sympathies to a woman on her husband's death, while failing to notice that she is not dressed in deep mourning?

VIOLET. *(Thunderstruck.)* What's that you say?

SHERLOCK. Not to mention being so slipshod in your research that you had failed to check your dates. Or to note that Mrs. Cyril Morton was not the only "Violet" mentioned in the accounts of my cases.

VIOLET. How could you know that? I mean, that I missed that? Did Mrs. Morton telephone you yesterday?

SHERLOCK. No, although you might have thought of that possibility before.

VIOLET. I don't understand. No one knows what happened in that sitting room except Mrs. Morton and Charles and myself.

SHERLOCK. And you never discussed it with this Charles, I suppose? He never offered you a word of rebuke afterwards? Gentle rebuke, I mean.

VIOLET. *(Deeply embarrassed.)* We did discuss it on the way home, of course. But I still don't understand your source for this devilish guesswork. We were quite alone in the cab.

SHERLOCK. You could hardly have been alone in a hired cab. Unless one of you brained the driver and took over the wheel yourself.

VIOLET. Oh, yes, well, the driver, of course. Deaf old codger with a heavy beard and a heavier brogue. He ... *(Suddenly the light dawns.)* Oh. I see. I had quite forgotten your famed mastery of disguise. Allow me to compliment you.

SHERLOCK. *(In the cabby's brogue.)* Think nothing of it, Miss. *(Returning to his own voice.)* As I said, I have no need of admiration in pursuit of my calling. Allow me to add that this Charles of yours seems a shallow piece of work.

VIOLET. Well, really! An impression formed on the basis of a bout of eavesdropping.

SHERLOCK. The method used does not invalidate the information gathered.

VIOLET. But you don't *know* him. He's very satisfactory on deeper acquaintance.

SHERLOCK. I see. Fully able to appreciate your intelligence and talent, is he? Supportive of your efforts?

VIOLET. In his way.

SHERLOCK. Blind to social pretension and possessed of enduring values? *(Violet is silent for quite a long while.)*

VIOLET. *(Quietly.)* The Great War did not leave behind many young men in my generation for the choosing.

SHERLOCK. That is true. Pray, forgive me.

VIOLET. *(Seizing the chance to change the subject.)* How then did you know I was going to visit Mrs. Morton?

SHERLOCK. I didn't know until I followed you.

VIOLET. *Followed* me?

SHERLOCK. I had a feeling you were going to take off up the wrong trail.

VIOLET. You mean that Mrs. Morton is not my mother.

SHERLOCK. I mean that searching for your mother is fruitless. There are other cases to investigate which could yield more satisfying results.

VIOLET. *(Tenacious.)* Then you didn't let Mrs. Morton know who I am?

SHERLOCK. I have not spoken with her. She put you off all on her own accord.

VIOLET. *(Bitterly.)* Yes, suspecting me as a mere fortune-hunter.

SHERLOCK. Well, you must understand ... a woman in her

position …

VIOLET.   You mean, a woman with a private fortune which she is unwilling to share any further?

SHERLOCK.   Now you are being uncharitable. I meant, rather, a woman whose husband is still, indeed, very much alive. If she had committed a past indiscretion …

VIOLET.   *(Finishing his thought.)* How would she react if that indiscretion, in the flesh, suddenly appeared in her sitting room. She would need to buy time to decide how to react. She would try to throw me temporarily off the trail.

SHERLOCK.   Not bad.

VIOLET.   So Irene Adler was just meant to throw me off the scent.

SHERLOCK.   *(Blanching.)* Who?

VIOLET.   Irene Adler. That's who I came here to ask you about.

SHERLOCK.   *(Still quite stunned.)* Mrs. Morton brought up the name of Irene Adler?

VIOLET.   *(Regarding him closely.)* Perhaps it was not a mere ploy on her part.

SHERLOCK.   *(Regaining his composure.)* Nonsense. Of course it was.

VIOLET.   Tell me about her.

SHERLOCK.   No.

VIOLET.   If she bears no true significance for you, you can hardly object. Can you? *(Sherlock realizes he is trapped. He cannot tell whether chagrin at his position is uppermost at this moment, or admiration at his daughter's cleverness in springing the trap.)* Can you?

SHERLOCK.   I suppose I cannot.

VIOLET.   Very well then.

SHERLOCK.   Where shall I begin?

VIOLET.   I have read *A Scandal in Bohemia*. In fact, I spent all of yesterday evening ensuring that my research would not be so 'slipshod' again. Perhaps you had best begin when the events of that adventure gave way to Miss Adler and her new husband's flight to the Continent. Followed not long after, if I may observe, by your journey to Switzerland and your own long sojourn abroad. *(Violet settles back, with a hint of triumph, to listen to her story. Sherlock shifts uncomfortably, then prepares to speak. As he tells the story we are transported in flashback to 1891. From offstage we hear a woman singing something operatic. As Sherlock remembers, he changes his clothing and steps into the scene.)*

SHERLOCK. *(Remembering.)* She had, of course, a lovely contralto voice — rich and clear and true. And I did not follow her nearly so soon as you imagine (you really must learn to pay more attention to chronology; it can be crucial). No, it was almost four years before I met Irene Adler again (for in spite of her marriage I can never think of her by any other name). I was commissioned by the French government to handle an affair of utmost delicacy. This occasioned my spending a great deal of time in France early in the year 1891. It was at this time I discovered she had taken up residence in Paris.

VIOLET. I thought she had died by that time — she and her husband both. A train wreck, wasn't it?

SHERLOCK. Oh no, she was very much alive. The train wreck story was put about to cover her trail, for the King of Bohemia was still interested in her whereabouts.

VIOLET. Did it succeed? The false story of her death?

SHERLOCK. Not entirely. For the King of Bohemia was no more inclined than I was to underestimate Miss Irene Adler. *(Irene Adler enters, resplendent in an afternoon gown of some kind. It is evident that his visit was unexpected and she has thrown on something appropriate for receiving visitors. She is a strikingly handsome woman with dark hair, quick-witted and possessed of great presence.)* Your man at the door is supposed to be a watchman, is he not? I might have been anyone and he'd have let me slip in.

IRENE. Why be just anyone when you could have presented yourself as ... Sherlock Holmes.

SHERLOCK. The one person I could not be, for reasons I dare not divulge. I am currently engaged by an important employer on a mission of great delicacy. It is necessary that I remain incognito.

IRENE. Ahh, deliciously mysterious.

SHERLOCK. You keep that aging pugilist at your door, no doubt, because you still wish to elude the agents of the King.

IRENE. Very astute, Mr. Holmes. I object to Willie's continued interest in my private affairs. Poor man, I fear he is rather confused now. According to the various reports he has recently received, I am either living scandalously apart from my husband, widowed, or dead myself. Then, of course, there is always the rumour that Godfrey and I are living happily ever after. I believe the King keeps sending people to find out which of the stories is true.

SHERLOCK. His agents shall learn nothing from me, it goes without saying.

IRENE. Thank you.

SHERLOCK. So you are perfectly safe in telling me which of the stories *is* true.

IRENE. *(Laughing brightly again.)* Well, Mr. Holmes, as you see, I am not dead.

SHERLOCK. Indeed not. *(Pause.)* Well … that leaves three other possibilities. Which of them is the truth?

IRENE. *(Teasingly.)* Can you not deduce? *(Sherlock is momentarily shy — rendered speechless by this outright flirtation.)* I must say, it is a great pleasure to meet you at last, face to face, with neither of us in disguise. I have long been your admirer.

SHERLOCK. May I say the feeling is mutual. Rarely have I been bested…. In fact, I believe you are the only person alive to hold that distinction. I take it, then, you are not widowed either? *(Irene's peignoir is not one that would suggest deep mourning.)*

IRENE. It is not easy to give you the slip, is it, Mr. Holmes? No, Godfrey is alive. His health has been delicate recently.

SHERLOCK. I am so sorry to hear it. Might I be permitted to pay my respects? *(Irene looks at him long and hard. There is a knowingness in her look, but also a searching.)*

IRENE. It is very kind of you, Mr. Holmes. But Godfrey is at present taking the waters at a spa, at the border of Switzerland and the Black Forest. The alpine air is thought to be beneficial for him.

SHERLOCK. Ahh. What a shame you could not accompany

him.

IRENE.   I go to join him at the end of the week.

SHERLOCK.   Travelling alone?

IRENE.   As needs must.

SHERLOCK.   My business takes me to Zurich shortly. Perhaps I could escort you to your destination.

IRENE.   A very courtly suggestion, Mr. Holmes. But one which could surely be misunderstood.

SHERLOCK.   Nonsense, Miss Adler, I am merely concerned to protect you from agents of the King. And I have no compunction about travelling in the guise of a serving man. The better to watch over you.

IRENE.   I see. You have made your deduction, then, between the two possibilities left.

SHERLOCK.   I have.

VIOLET.   So did you?

SHERLOCK.   *(Snapped back to the present suddenly.)* What?

VIOLET.   Did you go with her?

SHERLOCK.   Well, my dear ... *(Sherlock turns back to watch Irene vanish with another silvery laugh. Violet scarcely notices the reverie she has destroyed. She is hot on a trail of deductions.)*

VIOLET.   *(With growing excitement as she paints the picture.)* Of course you did. And then you developed a rendezvous place in Switzerland, where she could be near her convalescent husband, to keep his suspicions at bay. You went back to England and fetched Dr. Watson, and brought him along on a wild goose chase after Professor Moriarty. (Was he real, by the way, or did you invent him just for this purpose?) Then you staged your disappearance at the Reichenbach Falls, with Dr. Watson as witness, and were free to carry on your romantic sojourn in Switzerland while everyone believed you were dead. I must have been some kind of mistake or mishap — another reason for you both to stay incognito in the Alps until I was born. Then you placed me at that boarding school ... I gather money was no object with Irene married to a lawyer and pursued by kings. Are you with me?

SHERLOCK.   *(Drily.)* Pray, continue.

VIOLET.   You stayed in Switzerland just long enough to see

that I was well looked after. Then you determined that you could afford to make no such mistake again, given her marital status. So you parted, leaving arrangements in place to keep an eye on me. And you resurfaced dramatically in England in ...

SHERLOCK. 1894.

VIOLET. Thank you. Which means I must have been born in 1892 or 1893. It was clever of you to destroy the documentation. The lady in the veil and the man with the handlebar moustache, the great beard and the glasses — that was you, of course, in disguise. Irene returned to Paris with her husband and neither of you was ever in a position to contact me again.

SHERLOCK. Brava! Ably deduced.

VIOLET. Is there anything missing?

SHERLOCK. Facts. Witnesses.

VIOLET. Once the impossible has been eliminated what remains, however improbable, must be the truth. And you are my witness. So ... is it true?

SHERLOCK. It *is* improbable.

VIOLET. Well, I wasn't discovered under a cabbage leaf!

SHERLOCK. No, certainly not. But are you quite sure you have eliminated every possibility ... or impossibility?

VIOLET. Why won't you just *tell* me who my mother is?

SHERLOCK. Or was. I have my reasons.

VIOLET. Is she dead then? Why must you continue to protect the dead?

SHERLOCK. I did not say whether she was alive or dead. Indeed, what makes you so sure that I know?

VIOLET. I shall go mad!

SHERLOCK. *(Sharply.)* You had far better retain your sanity and engage in some sober investigative work with me. *(Pause.)* Well, if you are determined to pursue this end, surely there are other avenues of inquiry.

VIOLET. *(Struggling for calm.)* If I do not know who my mother is, how am I to determine whether she is alive or dead? And if I do not know whether she is alive or dead, how do I know what avenues of inquiry to pursue?

SHERLOCK. There is an obvious one you have not thought

of. Have you considered the science of spiritualism?

VIOLET.   What, communicating with the dead?

SHERLOCK.   Indeed, its practice has flourished recently thanks to the tragedies provided us by the Great War.

VIOLET.   Surely you don't believe —

SHERLOCK.   I don't believe in ruling out as unscientific forms of study which have yet to be fully researched. You wish to eliminate the impossible ... but how do you know it is impossible for us to contact the dead?

VIOLET.   I don't, but —

SHERLOCK.   Then you would be foolish to dismiss the potential information you might gain without at least checking.

VIOLET.   Do you know someone who engages in this ... table-rapping absurdity?

SHERLOCK.   I do. Whether you find it absurd remains to be seen. But I assure you, more than the rapping of tables is involved. There have been known to be actual apparitions.

VIOLET.   Do you mean that one can actually meet the departed spirit? *(Holmes lifts his eyebrow somewhat noncommittally, as if wishing to avoid casting pearls before swine.)* And you really know someone who is adept in these matters? *(A similar reaction from Holmes.)* In London, or here?

SHERLOCK.   London. You'll be close to home.

VIOLET.   Well, can it be arranged? You're right, I should remain open-minded. May I count on you to arrange it, then?

SHERLOCK.   I'll see what I can do.

VIOLET.   May I bring Charles?

SHERLOCK.   Why not? A certain earthbound presence in the room will lend credence to the proceedings. No point in having too many people there possessed of too much imagination.

Scene 5

We are in a moderately bohemian London sitting room decked with sheer curtains. A round table covered with a table-cloth and surrounded by four chairs is the main item of furniture. Selective lighting creates an atmosphere of mystery, bordering on the supernatural. Perhaps some eerie objects are present, which lend the place the air of a stage setting.

A bell rings offstage. Suddenly Turlough O'Brennan, the medium in residence, sweeps across the stage.

TURLOUGH. *(Calling offstage.)* Coming! Just a moment, please! *(He stops momentarily to straighten a lampshade or curtain. The bell rings again. He sweeps off, to answer the call. The back of his smoking jacket reveals a Celtic knot or some such appropriate design. Offstage.)* I'll be right with you! Just a moment! *(Arrival sounds — then Turlough ushers in Violet and Charles.)* Welcome, Miss Sheridan, Mr. Yorke. My name is Turlough O'Brennan. Are you ready to encounter the ineffable? Good, good. Make yourselves at home, if you would. I have a few last minute details to see to. *(Taking in their state, somewhat confidentially.)* It is most conducive, of course, if an atmosphere of calm and relaxation prevails. Do your best. I won't be a moment. *(And he's off again, leaving Violet and Charles alone like two children abandoned in the woods.)*

CHARLES. Gosh. It's all very well to *say* "Relax."

VIOLET. What do you think of the place, Charles?

CHARLES. Hmm? Oh, bit eerie for my taste. Well, I suppose that's the idea, isn't it? Still ...

VIOLET. That's not what I mean. Never mind the atmosphere ... is there anything that looks to you like a false panel in the wall? Or nooks where things could be concealed to make an effect? I wonder what sort of "last minute details" he has to see to.

CHARLES. Oh, yes ... I see what you mean. Good practice, this.

VIOLET.   What?

CHARLES.   Good sleuthing practice. In case you do help your father with that blackmail case.

VIOLET.   I'm not going to.

CHARLES.   Right. So you think this chap's not quite on the level?

VIOLET.   I don't know. I can't see my — my father consorting with someone who wasn't.

CHARLES.   Quite so. All these theatrics are just part of the business, aren't they?

VIOLET.   Hmm.

CHARLES.   Well, if you get to meet your mum face to face it'll all be worthwhile, won't it? Except, of course, that'll mean she's dead.

VIOLET.   If I learned nothing else, Charles, from our encounter with Mrs. Morton, I learned not to attach too much importance to one desired outcome. Let the truth be what it is. It's simply up to us to find it. If we let our emotions lead us astray — well, the truth will make fools of us, won't it?

CHARLES.   Still, I do hope it's nothing shameful or scandalous.

VIOLET.   How can it *not* be? Or why would he go to such lengths to dissuade me from finding out?

CHARLES.   Now, Violet. You're not being quite fair to the strong sex, you know.

VIOLET.   Am I not?

CHARLES.   A gentleman has to protect a lady. Especially one for whom he has tender feelings. Sometimes promises are made which may not be broken. We don't know what might have passed between them so many years ago — what vows, what agreements. I think your father is behaving absolutely first class in all this. He's come up with a way for you to find the information without him having to divulge it himself. It's quite brilliant, now that I think of it. The old boy doesn't have a deceptive bone in his body. So he's found a gentle, fatherly way to satisfy your curiosity while remaining true to his bargains. Marvellous! *(Just at this moment a workman enters from the back room. He is grimy and a bit sweaty, and speaks with a thick*

Cockney accent.)

WORKMAN. 'Scuse me, sir. Miss. D'ye 'appen to know where a bloke could wash 'is 'ands?

CHARLES. I'm sorry, my good man. We're guests here and don't know the lay-out, if you know what I mean. Why don't you ask 'mein host'?

WORKMAN. Oh, that wouldn't do, sir. 'E's much too busy flittin' about. Between you and me and the fence-post, I think a common wash-basin might be a bit too earthly for 'im to locate, if you know what I mean. *(Workman mimes a spritzing gesture, as of one substituting cologne for hygiene.)*

VIOLET. I'm sorry, we're not able to direct you. If you turned your powers of observation from our host to the house itself you might be able to find a wash-basin without our assistance.

WORKMAN. Oh, I've been observing 'ouse and master alike, Miss, don't you worry. Lot can go on in an establishment like this, you mark my words.

CHARLES. Well, we rather hope so. That's why we're here.

WORKMAN. Very understandable, young sir. All the same, keep yer eyes an' ears open. Fings may not be wot they seem. Crikey, I could certainly use a spot to doff some of these dusty things. *(Quite unexpectedly he begins to remove his clothes, much to Charles's alarm.)*

CHARLES. Oh, I say!

VIOLET. Sir, we shall be obliged to call for — *(However, once the workman pulls the hair off his own head and wipes some grime from his face, he is clearly revealed to be Sherlock Holmes.)*

SHERLOCK. As I said, things may not be what they seem.

VIOLET. *(Wryly.)* Mr. Charles Wellington Yorke ... I should like you to meet my father, Mr. Sherlock Holmes.

CHARLES. Great Scot! I mean, how do you do, sir? I've been a great admirer of yours since I was in knee pan —

SHERLOCK. *(Cutting him off.)* Thank you. Now, in all earnestness, do please help me find a washbasin before I am quite discovered.

VIOLET. What have you been up to?

SHERLOCK. Checking the house over. To see whether Mr.

O'Brennan's establishment boasts any hidden panels, projection screens or any other such trickery.

CHARLES. I say, what a splendid idea!

VIOLET. And?

SHERLOCK. I have found none. Mr. O'Brennan seems to be a sincere practitioner of his art ... a rare breed. Let us hope he actually possesses the special powers he claims and that we shall not spend a fruitless evening. Now, Violet, you stay here in case Mr. O'Brennan should return suddenly. Mr. Yorke, I shall ask you to come with me and assist in disposing with these. Then we will return as if you had answered the front door and let me in, in the absence of our host. *(The two men exit hurriedly, leaving Violet. She touches a few objects, like the table and curtains, to assure herself of their reality and solidity. Turlough returns, catching her unawares and causing her to jump a little.)*

TURLOUGH. Miss Sheridan — Oh, I'm so sorry to have startled you. You are alone?

VIOLET. Oh. Yes. Charles, that is Mr. Yorke, heard the bell at the front door and since you seemed occupied, he has gone to see who it might be.

TURLOUGH. Splendid! No doubt Mr. Holmes ... our fourth for bridge, as it were. *(Violet tries to muster a laugh for this jest, and is saved by the return of Charles and Holmes.)* Mr. Holmes! Your timing is excellent. Everything is prepared. The curtain is ready to rise. *(Noting Violet's discomfort.)* I mean, of course, Miss Sheridan, the curtain of illusion which separates this world from the next. *(In Gaelic.)* Scathain istigh scathain; doras taobh thall doras.*

SHERLOCK. *(Translating.)* 'Mirrors within mirrors; doors beyond doors.' Gaelic. Mr. O'Brennan is a member of the Order of the Golden Dawn, the organization your Mr. Yeats became part of when he began his spiritualist researches. *(Turlough gives a bow of such exaggerated modesty that one might think he had held the very hand of the poet himself at many a seance.)*

*See A Note from the Author for pronunciation.

TURLOUGH. *(Portentously.)* Well. Shall we begin. I will ask you to sit, please, and take hands. *(They sit. Turlough dims the lights slightly then joins them.)* Allow me a moment to focus my energies. I will ask all of you to concentrate on the task at hand. We are attempting, as I understand, to commune with the spirit of this young lady's deceased mother? Or to gain news of her, if she is alive, through friends in the spirit world. Close your eyes, please, one and all, and concentrate. *(Everyone does so, and therefore misses seeing Turlough enter into a trance-like swaying. His eyes roll up in his head and his mouth begins to open and move as if to speak. We see Violet's and Charles's hands tightening in one another's grip so that they lift off the table. Sherlock looks calm and focused. From some indefinable source we begin to hear music — unearthly and mysterious.)* I feel a spirit approaching us. Come closer, wanderer in the astral realms! Here you will find only friends, who wish your well-being. *(A woman's voice is heard singing — something classical, perhaps operatic. The light behind one of the sheer curtains U. becomes faintly more luminous. A figure appears ... hard to distinguish at first. She is singing in a clear contralto voice. She wears a dazzling 1890's gown and has a wealth of dark hair. To the table, sotto voce.)* You may open your eyes very slowly, but on no account must you let go of one another's hands or the connection will be lost. *(To the apparition.)* Come forward, spirit. Do you have news to share with us? *(The spirit answers with a silvery laugh. Something in the room goes flying.)*

VIOLET. *(Under her breath, to Charles.)* Oh, God!

CHARLES. What is it, darling?

VIOLET. The voice, the singing.... It's that Irene Adler woman, it must be!

CHARLES. Oh, dear. Do you think she's ...

TURLOUGH. Speak to us in a human voice! You have not forgotten. *(A light blows out. Turlough seems to be engaged in a battle of wills with the mischievous spirit.)* Tell me, do you know anyone in this room? *(This merits only another peal of laughter and another bright aria.)* By the source of eternal light, I charge you: Do you know anyone in this circle?

IRENE. *(In a faraway voice.)* Yes.

36

TURLOUGH.   Who do you know? *(More laughter is the response, and a snatch of melody.)* I charge you, answer me! Do you know Mr. Sherlock Holmes?

IRENE.   Yes.

TURLOUGH.   Do you know this young gentleman?

IRENE.   No.

TURLOUGH.   Do you know this young lady?

IRENE.   I know who she is.

TURLOUGH.   Do you have any relationship with anyone sitting in this room? *(At this the spirit seems unable to contain her mischievous laughter.)* Answer me!

IRENE.   Not until Mr. Holmes removes that prim expression from around his mouth. *(Sherlock, more than a little chagrinned, seeks to adjust his body position as well as his face.)*

TURLOUGH.   Did you, in life, have any intimate relationship with this gentleman?

IRENE.   How can one answer such a question? What feels intimate to one, another experiences as distance.

TURLOUGH.   You answer me in riddles.

IRENE.   Your question poses one of life's greatest riddles. What a relief it is to be free of it! And free of one's ties!

TURLOUGH.   Some ties last beyond life, even beyond death. Let me ask you plainly, then: Are you this young lady's mother? *(There is no answer at first. The light behind the curtain seems to dim.)*

SHERLOCK.   Irene, I beg you. Her peace of mind depends upon it. For my sake, answer. *(No answer yet.)*

TURLOUGH.   I ask you again: Are you this young lady's mother?

IRENE.   I know who is. *(The light begins to fade on her in earnest. If her visitation has been accompanied by any background sound it begins to fade.)*

TURLOUGH.   Stay, I charge you! You may yet be able to help us. Do not leave this young soul disappointed. You say you know who her mother is?

IRENE.   I do.

TURLOUGH.   Can you prevail upon her to visit us? *(He is answered only by wavering light.)*

SHERLOCK. Irene, be kind. Help us.

IRENE. Help you?

SHERLOCK. You were always the most admirable of women. Prove so now.

IRENE. Does the young lady wish it?

CHARLES. Violet?

VIOLET. *(Barely able to speak.)* I do wish it. Please, Miss Adler, I do.

IRENE. Let me see what I can do. *(Irene begins to sing again, but this time the effect is less mischievous. There is more a sense of yearning in the melody, the effect being that she seems to be calling to someone on another channel of communication. The curtains begin to blow a bit, and the lighting changes again. Sherlock sniffs the air like a hound on a scent.)*

SHERLOCK. There. Do you notice?

CHARLES. *(Sniffing.)* Oh, I say!

VIOLET. The scent of violets. *(Another figure starts to materialize behind the curtain, with Irene. This apparition is once again a woman in 1890's garb — but her face is thickly veiled. Sherlock is at the edge of his seat ... and he is not the only one.)*

TURLOUGH. Approach, spirit. Tell us who you are. *(The apparition slowly shakes her head.)*

IRENE. She will not speak.

TURLOUGH. Can you speak for her?

IRENE. I can.

TURLOUGH. Spirit, are you this young woman's mother? *(Irene looks at the woman, who slowly nods her veiled head.)*

IRENE. She answers 'Yes.'

TURLOUGH. In life, how were you known?

IRENE. *(Looking to woman for her cue.)* 'I was known, by some, as Agatha.'

TURLOUGH. Where did you meet Mr. Sherlock Holmes?

IRENE. *(Interpreting.)* 'At the home of Charles Augustus Milverton.'

TURLOUGH. What was the occasion of your acquaintance with Mr. Holmes?

IRENE. *(Interpreting.)* 'I helped him gain access to the house.'

TURLOUGH. Were you a guest there?

38

IRENE.   *(Interpreting.)* 'No.'

TURLOUGH.   A daughter of the house? A relative?

IRENE.   *(Interpreting.)* 'No.'

TURLOUGH.   What then?

IRENE.   *(Interpreting.)* 'I was in service there.'

TURLOUGH.   A housemaid?

IRENE.   *(Still interpreting.)* 'Yes.'

CHARLES.   *(Under his breath.)* Oh, I say!

IRENE.   *(Still interpreting.)* 'Mr. Holmes came disguised as a tradesman. He desired to become engaged to me. Little did I know who he was or that he had other matters afoot in the house. I gave him what help I could and in return —' *(Suddenly Violet jumps up and flees the room, headed for the outside door. Immediately the lights behind the U. curtains dim and the apparitions disappear. The men look after her, and then at one another.)*

END OF ACT ONE

ACT TWO

Scene 1

Violet's studio. Violet is working on a clay model. She may not have slept much this weekend, and is somewhat careless of her appearance. She practically flings clay at the model, working with an intensity that borders on the ferocious.

Sounds of footsteps offstage. Charles appears, somewhat hesitant and nervous. She does not hear him at first. He clears his throat.

VIOLET.   Charles!

CHARLES.   Good afternoon.

VIOLET.   Is it?

CHARLES.   Is it good?

VIOLET.   Is it afternoon? I didn't know.

CHARLES.   Ahh.

VIOLET.   *(Stirring herself.)* All the same, I'm glad to see you. Give us a kiss. *(He does so — but just a peck.)* Well, that was cheery.

CHARLES.   *(Trying to do better.)* Sorry. Didn't want you to catch my cold.

VIOLET.   Oh, have you got a cold? Poor lamb! Let me make you some tea. Would you like that?

CHARLES.   Planning to use hot water, are you?

VIOLET.   Yes, I think I will this time. Tea, then?

CHARLES.   Umm, no, there's no need.

VIOLET.   Oh. All right.... Haven't seen you for a few days.

CHARLES.   Yes, I know. Sorry.

VIOLET.   I suppose you thought I needed some time to myself. *(Pause.)* Or did you need some time to yourself?

CHARLES.   Well. Yes, I did, rather.

VIOLET.   Oh. I see.

CHARLES.   Well, *you* know ...

VIOLET.   Your cold, I suppose?

CHARLES.   Yes, that — and ... *(She refuses to answer — simply watches him. Long pause.)* Quite a revelation, all in all.

VIOLET.   Yes.

CHARLES.   I mean ... one wouldn't have guessed —

VIOLET.   *(Sharply.)* What? That I'm a bastard or that I'm common?

CHARLES.   *(Stunned.)* Violet, I —

VIOLET.   Oh, Charles, you *are* a pig! *(Pause.)*

CHARLES.   Yes, that was rather piggish of me, wasn't it? *(Pause.)* I'm sorry, darling. *(Violet lets go suddenly and melts into his arms.)*

VIOLET.   Never mind, darling. The important thing is, you're here! Can you imagine how silly I was? When I didn't see you after that awful séance, when you didn't come after me, I started to think maybe you weren't going to come. And after a day or two I really believed I wasn't going to see you again. I really thought you weren't going to come — but you're here! You're here, and that's all that matters.

CHARLES.   *(Weakly.)* Yes, yes. There now, there now.

VIOLET.   And we'll think of something to say to your bloody old parents, we'll think of something that will make it all right. They can't be as rigid as all that. They'll just have to understand, that's all. They'll just have to find it within themselves to understand. And everything will be all right. *(Pause.)* Won't it, darling? *(Long pause.)* Won't it? *(Charles can't answer. Slowly Violet detaches herself from him and looks at him very deeply.)* It's not going to work, is it?

CHARLES.   I'm afraid not.

VIOLET.   They won't understand, will they?

CHARLES.   No. *(Pause.)*

VIOLET.   Well. That's that, then.

CHARLES.   I really have to be —

VIOLET.   Going, yes.

CHARLES.   Sorry.

VIOLET.   Well then —

CHARLES.   I did just ...

VIOLET.   What?

41

CHARLES. *(Awkwardly.)* I did just wonder if I might ... have back that silver vase I brought over once.

VIOLET. Oh, I see.

CHARLES. I know you'll think I'm being piggish again. It's just that it's been in the family for generations. I shall have to account for it at some point — *(Violet pulls out the flowers Charles brought the other day and flings them to the floor. She tosses the vase to [or rather, at] him.)*

VIOLET. Anything else?

CHARLES. Violet, I —

VIOLET. Because I don't ever want to see you again — not ever!

CHARLES. Please under —

VIOLET. Get out! Just *go!* (*Charles, unable to think of an alternative, turns and goes. When she is quite sure he's gone, Violet flings herself back at the model, hurling clay between sobs. After some moments we hear footsteps again. Violet rouses herself to call over her shoulder.)* I have nothing to say to you! Go away! *(The footsteps stop. She returns to her work. Silently someone enters the room. It is Sherlock Holmes. He is not in good health. He surveys the scene.)*

SHERLOCK. I told you you could do better.

VIOLET. *(Turning her head suddenly.)* What?

SHERLOCK. He wasn't worthy of you.

VIOLET. What makes you think —

SHERLOCK. Oh, come now. *(He indicates the flowers on the floor, the disarray in the studio, and a tear in the corner of her eye.)*

VIOLET. You're quite right, of course. No point in pretending.

SHERLOCK. Bad luck, all the same.

VIOLET. I have nothing to say to you either. Please go. *(Sherlock sits.)*

SHERLOCK. You needn't say anything. I've a few things to say to you.

VIOLET. I should think.

SHERLOCK. Are you willing to listen? *(Violet stops and stares at him, but does not go as far as to sit down or display a real commitment to conversing.)* No doubt you are somewhat disappointed by the revelations of the other evening. *(Violet gives a short, cyni-*

42

cal laugh.) It seems your young man was even more keenly disappointed. *(He elicits no response from her on this.)* Have you thought what you will do now?

VIOLET.   I scarcely know what to do.

SHERLOCK.   Your art —

VIOLET.   I believe I may say, without slighting my own talent, that the interest Charles's family showed in me was a factor in securing the exhibition for me.

SHERLOCK.   Surely it has given you enough of a start that you can make your own way now.

VIOLET.   Perhaps. But you came to tell me some things. Once again you are asking.

SHERLOCK.   Ah, well —

VIOLET.   Perhaps you wished to shed some light on the circumstances of my conception and birth.

SHERLOCK.   No.

VIOLET.   *(Dismissively.)* Well then —

SHERLOCK.   I did ask you, recently, whether you might be interested in investigating a case with me. But ...

VIOLET.   But?

SHERLOCK.   Perhaps I should think better of that idea.

VIOLET.   Oh. Because the respectable presence of your Dr. Watson is more suitable to you than that of an illegitimate working class companion?

SHERLOCK.   Those things are hardly factors.

VIOLET.   I'm sorry, I should have said 'daughter' rather than companion. *(A light goes on.)* Or should I have said 'daughter' rather than 'son'? *(Long pause.)* Perhaps it's because I'm a woman that you would find my assistance irrelevant.

SHERLOCK.   A woman, yes. And an inexperienced one.

VIOLET.   Well! So my personal capabilities are irrelevant because of my sex. I thought you considered my artistic sense of observation closely related to your own.

SHERLOCK.   Well, with training, I suppose —

VIOLET.   My intelligence, my capacity to deduce — my God, even my faculty of curiosity — are rendered irrelevant by my gender.

SHERLOCK.   What can I say?

43

VIOLET.   Am I not of your blood, even if I don't happen to be a son? Am I not your daughter?

SHERLOCK.   Well. We shall see.

VIOLET.   We certainly bloody will!

SHERLOCK.   *(Wryly.)* Allow me then to tell you a little about the case. *(Violet realizes, at last, that she has been drawn in, in spite of herself. She settles down to take up her "fate.")* It has taken a very serious turn.

VIOLET.   The blackmail case —

SHERLOCK.   Has become murder.

VIOLET.   When?

SHERLOCK.   The day before yesterday. The man in question was a rather prominent politician, Lord Carrington.

VIOLET.   The Colonial Secretary!

SHERLOCK.   Indeed. Found dead in his home. No trace of violence; his heart simply stopped.

VIOLET.   A heart attack?

SHERLOCK.   Scotland Yard thinks not. None of the symptoms one would expect.

VIOLET.   Poison.

SHERLOCK.   It could be. Although an extremely sophisticated one. He was found in his favourite drawing room chair. On the table next to him a sherry decanter and two glasses. One had been drunk from, the other not.

VIOLET.   Something in the sherry, clearly.

SHERLOCK.   I'm afraid not. No trace.

VIOLET.   Do we know who his companion was?

SHERLOCK.   According to the servants, he typically took a glass of sherry with his wife around five o'clock.

VIOLET.   Did she usually drink?

SHERLOCK.   Yes.

VIOLET.   And his time of death?

SHERLOCK.   Between five and six.

VIOLET.   Seems rather obvious.

SHERLOCK.   Except that we know of no motive. And have no witnesses to the wife's arrival in or departure from the drawing room. Remember, too — this started as a blackmail case.

VIOLET. Which means?

SHERLOCK. Which means that someone else might have had a motive.

VIOLET. But who?

SHERLOCK. Exactly.

VIOLET. With what information was Lord Carrington being blackmailed?

SHERLOCK. It was *Lady* Carrington who was being blackmailed.

VIOLET. *(Wrapping her mind around this.)* Lady Carrington as blackmail victim leads to Lord Carrington as murder victim.... What is the next step, then?

SHERLOCK. The next step is for you to go and interview the deceased's wife. See whether you can elicit any information that might shed some light.

VIOLET. Why send me? Why not go yourself?

SHERLOCK. There can be, after all, some advantages in being a woman. And one who is —

VIOLET. Inexperienced?

SHERLOCK. Shall we say, not well known.

VIOLET. Have Scotland Yard asked you to assist with the case?

SHERLOCK. *(Strained.)* No. They have not.

VIOLET. Why not? *(She receives no answer.)* Is it because they do not wish you to come out of retirement?

SHERLOCK. Perhaps.

VIOLET. And you think that sending me will make your participation in the case inconspicuous to them?

SHERLOCK. There is another reason. *(Violet waits.)* I told you that my health is not what it was.... Some of the rigours of investigation take a heavier toll than ... than they did in the past.

VIOLET. You need a surrogate.

SHERLOCK. *(Flaring.)* There is nothing wrong with my powers of deduction! They are as keen as ever, perhaps keener. I need ... a pair of eyes. *(Long pause.)*

VIOLET. I will help you. *(Sherlock accepts this with a grace that is more than tinged with wryness.)*

SHERLOCK. Thank you. *(Pause.)* There is something else.

VIOLET. Oh?

SHERLOCK. Lady Carrington approached me to help her with this case. Yet she has been less than entirely frank with me.

VIOLET. Do you mean that she has lied?

SHERLOCK. She won't tell me what happened when she arrived home on the day of the murder.

VIOLET. And you think she will tell me?

SHERLOCK. That is what I'm hoping.

VIOLET. Well, what shall I say to her that might persuade her to speak?

SHERLOCK. I see what you mean. Well.... Tell her you are my daughter.

Scene 2

London. Violet is ushered into a rather stately drawing room with high ceilings and high windows. Lady Carrington awaits her.

LADY CARRINGTON. Miss — Sheridan?

VIOLET. Yes.

LADY CARRINGTON. You are Mr. Holmes's —

VIOLET. *(Hesitating.)* Associate.

LADY CARRINGTON. I see.

VIOLET. He very much regrets that his health does not permit him to call upon you personally.

LADY CARRINGTON. Of course. I understand. *(Pause.)*

VIOLET. May I ask you a few questions about the day of your husband's death?

LADY CARRINGTON. You may ask.

VIOLET. Thank you. Now if I may begin with the facts as related by Scotland Yard.... It was your custom to take a glass of sherry with Lord Carrington in this room between five and

46

six o'clock. On the evening in question two glasses were set but only one was poured. You raised an alarm at quarter past six. The servants came. Your husband was found dead — no sign of violence or forcible entry into the room. Just you ... and one glass drained of sherry.

LADY CARRINGTON.   Yes, I quite see how the picture appears.

VIOLET.   What happened in this room between five o'clock and quarter past six?

LADY CARRINGTON.   I cannot account for all that time. I arrived just before six. I was late.

VIOLET.   The servants were unaware of your late arrival?

LADY CARRINGTON.   We did not encourage them to hover around us at that hour. It was our one island of private calm together in the middle of a hectic schedule.

VIOLET.   But surely one of them would have taken your hat when you arrived at the door.

LADY CARRINGTON.   I came in through the French windows.

VIOLET.   In this room?

LADY CARRINGTON.   Yes.

VIOLET.   And placed your hat...?

LADY CARRINGTON.   I was not wearing one.

VIOLET.   Where had you been? *(Pause.)*

LADY CARRINGTON.   I prefer not to say.

VIOLET.   That is why you were unable to account for your movements to Scotland Yard?

LADY CARRINGTON.   I did not lie to them. I simply did not answer their questions.

VIOLET.   I see. And will you answer mine?

LADY CARRINGTON.   On that subject, no. I do not believe so. *(Pause.)*

VIOLET.   Lady Carrington, I need hardly tell you this represents a serious impediment to my ability to help you.

LADY CARRINGTON.   I understand, yes. But I have not asked you to help me.

VIOLET.   You asked Mr. Holmes.

LADY CARRINGTON.   That is a different matter.

VIOLET.   Not so very different.

LADY CARRINGTON.   I'm sorry. I don't understand what you mean.

VIOLET.   *(Screwing up her courage.)* I am Mr. Holmes's daughter. *(Long pause.)*

LADY CARRINGTON.   That isn't possible.

VIOLET.   Why not?

LADY CARRINGTON.   I didn't know that Mr. Holmes was married. *(This embarrasses Violet, who doesn't know how to respond. Lady Carrington continues somewhat harshly.)* Why did he send you to me?

VIOLET.   To see if you would answer my questions about what happened during that hour. Will you?

LADY CARRINGTON.   *(Furious.)* No. *(Lady Carrington begins to pace restlessly. Violet scans the room, looking for any kind of clues or details that might help. Everything seems in order.)*

VIOLET.   Lady Carrington, is there nothing you can tell me which will help support your innocence? No trail of inquiry for me to pursue?

LADY CARRINGTON.   *(Still agitated.)* Yes, all right. As I approached the house I saw a man stealing away from this room.

VIOLET.   Through the French windows?

LADY CARRINGTON.   Yes. They were never locked during the day.

VIOLET.   Can you describe him?

LADY CARRINGTON.   Tall. Solidly built. Dark hair. He had a huge handlebar moustache — so large I couldn't help thinking it might be a false one.

VIOLET.   Agile?

LADY CARRINGTON.   He moved well enough.

VIOLET.   He didn't see you?

LADY CARRINGTON.   I had no wish to draw attention to myself.

VIOLET.   And that is why, no doubt, you failed to mention him to Scotland Yard.

LADY CARRINGTON.   I could hardly do so without drawing attention to my own unorthodox route of return.

VIOLET.   This sudden revelation is all very convenient, Lady

Carrington, but how am I to believe you? *(Lady Carrington stares at Violet.)*

LADY CARRINGTON.   You must believe me because it is true.

VIOLET.   You will forgive me for saying so, Lady Carrington, but there is no real reason why blackmail should have led to murder in this case. Surely you and Lord Carrington were in a position to handle any financial demands that might be placed upon you, and there an end of the matter.

LADY CARRINGTON.   *(With a cynical laugh.)* There are two things you do not take into account.

VIOLET.   And those are?

LADY CARRINGTON.   My husband's character. He was not one to ... cooperate in such a situation.

VIOLET.   And the other? *(Pause.)*

LADY CARRINGTON.   Perhaps you cannot fully imagine what it feels like to be blackmailed. I sincerely hope you have not had the occasion to find out.

VIOLET.   You are right, Lady Carrington. I have not been privileged to have that experience.

LADY CARRINGTON.   I'm glad to hear it. I experienced it when I was a young woman — probably your age. You look surprised, Miss Sheridan, and you are right. That I should experience blackmail twice in one lifetime makes my current situation all the more bitter.

VIOLET.   What could anyone possibly have held over you when you were my age?

LADY CARRINGTON.   A great deal. I doubt that, in your generation, an unseemly revelation could ruin a girl's marriage prospects.

VIOLET.   You might be surprised.

LADY CARRINGTON.   *(Looking deeply at her.)* Is that so?

In my generation it was a tyranny. You see, it was not enough to be respectable ... a young woman had to be spotless. To behave improperly was out of the question. But even to think improperly exposed one to danger. And if one were mad enough to commit one's thoughts to paper ...

I was mad enough. A young man used to visit my father's

home. It was understood that if a young man continued to visit a home containing a young woman, he had a serious intent. I scarcely cared about intent, because he came bearing books of poetry — often with a wildflower pressed at a certain page, so that when I was alone I could read and divine his most secret thoughts. And I began to signal to him. He would take home the gift of a book from me, and rose petals from our garden would tumble out of some specially significant page. My father watched him closely, and made some inquiries into his family and prospects. I watched him closely in my own way. Never had I made such a study of a face, of a fall of hair over a brow....

We had little privacy, and no freedom to speak. Even inner freedom, I mean. Tongue-tied. We could only choose poets who would speak for us, and mark their pages.

Then one Sunday afternoon my father announced my engagement ... to someone I had scarcely met. My young man had no future, he said. And he was no longer welcome to call at our house. This new beau had breeding, money, a start on a brilliant political career. The matter was settled.

Suddenly, I was no longer tongue-tied. I couldn't speak out to my father, of course — but I could write. I could write what no poet could express for me ... and I wrote obsessively to my young man. My father would have been shocked, I think, to know what poured out of me — feelings he could never imagine his daughter experiencing.

It was this flood of freedom that placed me in the power of an unscrupulous monster.

My letters fell into his hands — just how, I will never know. Although I will always entertain the nightmare fear that they were placed there, for motives of profit. *(With bitterness.)* By whom ... I dare not speculate. Suffice to say, this man gave me notice in writing that my upcoming marriage and my very reputation could be saved only by the payment of a sum of money far greater than I could imagine, much less obtain.

VIOLET. Did this creature prey only on women? Surely there must have been young men who faced their wedding days with scandal behind them.

LADY CARRINGTON. Oh, indeed. Young men were almost expected to commit some indiscretions before marriage. And after, of course, was their own concern. It was all the more reason they must marry stainless women. They bathed themselves in us as in a purifying river, and emerged blameless. A man's soul could be as black as soot, as long as his wife's appeared white.

VIOLET. I take it your reputation was saved, since you achieved a brilliant match.

LADY CARRINGTON. Yes, Lord Carrington was certainly a brilliant match.

VIOLET. And with your soul appearing white again, his could afford to be a little black?

LADY CARRINGTON. *(Wary.)* I'm not sure what you're driving at. *(Pause.)*

VIOLET. Was your marriage a happy one, Lady Carrington? *(Pause.)*

LADY CARRINGTON. Thank you for your interest in the case, Miss Sheridan, but I have other pressing matters to attend to.

VIOLET. I haven't —

LADY CARRINGTON. If anything else comes to mind, I'll let you know.

VIOLET. I see. Well. Thank you, Lady Carrington.

LADY CARRINGTON. And remember ...

VIOLET. Yes?

LADY CARRINGTON. Not to judge anything too hastily. *(Lady Carrington ushers Violet out. Then for a moment she turns upstage and stares in thought. We follow Violet out into the street before the house. She stops and takes a deep breath. Two figures cross her path: a tall man and a veiled lady. They do not notice Violet at first; they seem to be regarding the Carrington house intently. They turn to one another and begin an intense conversation, which we cannot hear. The conversation becomes heated. The veiled lady's back is to Violet, but the man is clearly visible. It is Turlough O'Brennan. In the heat of the argument, he lifts the lady's veil, as if to confront her violently. Violet cannot help rushing forward.)*

51

VIOLET.   Mr. O'Brennan! *(The man stops and stares at Violet, frozen. Then he speaks, with no trace of an Irish accent.)*
MAN.   I'm sorry, Miss. You must be mistaken.
VIOLET.   *(Confused.)* But ... aren't you Turlough O'Brennan? I met you only a few days ago. *(From under the lady's hat a familiar voice emerges: deep and rich.)*
LADY.   Jack, you'd better set the young lady straight.
MAN.   My name is John Barton, Miss, late of the Lyceum. At your service. *(He gives a courtly bow, which Violet scarcely notices because the now unveiled lady has turned to face her. It is Irene Adler. Before Violet can catch her breath, the two turn and disappear down the street.)*
VIOLET.   *(Almost under her breath.)* Irene Adler ...

Scene 3

Mrs. Morton's drawing room. Violet enters, explaining over her shoulder to the maid:

VIOLET.   No, she isn't expecting me but I'll announce myself. Thank you — there's no need. *(Evidently drawn by the sound of this small commotion, Mrs. Morton enters from her music room.)*
MRS. MORTON.   *(Surprised.)* Miss Sheridan!
VIOLET.   Mrs. Morton, forgive my bursting in on you like this. But it is a matter of utmost urgency.
MRS. MORTON.   I see.
VIOLET.   *(Sitting.)* When last we met you mentioned the name of Irene Adler.
MRS. MORTON.   *(Guarded.)* Yes.
VIOLET.   You alluded to the fact that she might be alive.
MRS. MORTON.   Did I?
VIOLET.   You did, Mrs. Morton. And you were right. I need to know how to get in touch with her.

MRS. MORTON.   What gives you the idea that I would know —

VIOLET.   Have you spoken with Mr. Holmes recently?

MRS. MORTON.   *(A little off balance.)* I? Why, no.

VIOLET.   Then you have spoken with Irene Adler.

MRS. MORTON.   Really, I don't see how you —

VIOLET.   You greeted me just now as Miss Sheridan. But when I met you last, I introduced myself as Miss Hunter. Since then you have spoken with someone who knows who I am.

MRS. MORTON.   *(Unable to deny it.)* Ahh.

VIOLET.   And you knew that Irene Adler was alive. Something that not everyone is aware of. You must be keeping track of her, whatever your reasons may be.

MRS. MORTON.   That is very impressive, Miss Sheridan.

VIOLET.   Never mind whether it is impressive. Is it true? *(Pause.)*

MRS. MORTON.   I have spoken with Miss Adler.

VIOLET.   She contacted you?

MRS. MORTON.   I contacted her.

VIOLET.   Upon what occasion?

MRS. MORTON.   The occasion of your last visit here.

VIOLET.   *(Surprised.)* Really?

MRS. MORTON.   *(Choosing her words carefully.)* Your visit raised some questions from the past which ... which needed to be pursued. For my peace of mind.

VIOLET.   Questions involving Irene Adler?

MRS. MORTON.   Partly.

VIOLET.   Involving Sherlock Holmes.

MRS. MORTON.   Partly.

VIOLET.   You knew of a relationship between them.

MRS. MORTON.   I suspected.

VIOLET.   You could only have known such a thing if you yourself were close to Mr. Holmes. You were jealous.

MRS. MORTON.   Oh, Miss Sheridan —

VIOLET.   And your jealousy is such that any effort to uncover Mr. Holmes's — family relations is abhorrent to you. You would thwart any such attempt if you could.

MRS. MORTON.   No, there you are quite wrong.

VIOLET. Am I? If a piece of information could have an impact on someone else's happiness, you would withhold it, because of your own unhappiness.

MRS. MORTON. You misunderstand me, Miss Sheridan. *(She begins to move back into the past.)* Strange. You are not the first to so misunderstand me.

VIOLET. What do you mean?

MRS. MORTON. As I mentioned to you, I did become — friends with Mr. Holmes ... after the adventure recounted by Dr. Watson. He was not an easy man to draw close to, as I am sure you are aware. *(As she speaks, Mrs. Morton is drawn back in her memory and becomes the young Violet Smith again. Sherlock Holmes enters the scene, also as he was 20 years earlier.)*

VIOLET SMITH. *(To Sherlock.)* If your attention is drawn elsewhere, what can I do but accept it?

SHERLOCK. My attention is drawn always and absorbingly by my work — as you well know.

VIOLET SMITH. That is not what I am referring to.

SHERLOCK. *(Guarded.)* What can you mean?

VIOLET SMITH. Can you not deduce? Will you oblige me to spell it out...?

SHERLOCK. My dear Violet.... What evidence have you — ?

VIOLET SMITH. A woman's intuition is no less keen than your own. And there is the small matter of an exceptional bill ... at a lady's milliner. For a hat and some rather fine lace. *(She lifts the said bill from a place of concealment.)*

SHERLOCK. Inconclusive at best. And why the devil have you been snooping amongst my things?

VIOLET SMITH. I was looking to retrieve my note to you, which had come to seem ... overwritten in light of the coolness of your response.

SHERLOCK. Nonsense. Your note was charming and if mine lacked charm ... no doubt I was distracted in the writing of it. And a bill from a lady's milliner could relate to any one of the cases I am currently pursuing.

VIOLET SMITH. To the theft of a set of admiralty plans? Or the deciphering of a code based on stick figures? *(Shaking her head.)* No. Eliminate the impossible and what remains, however improbable, must be the truth.

SHERLOCK. It is singularly unpleasant to have one's own words flung in one's teeth.

VIOLET SMITH. There are others I could use ... words which have passed between us, which now seem to hold no meaning. Must I?

SHERLOCK. No. Such cruelty is not required.

VIOLET SMITH. *You* speak of cruelty. *(Pause.)*

SHERLOCK. Violet, you know that I am no sort of a prospect as a man. Never was. Were it not for your qualities, your beauty ... I would not have —

VIOLET SMITH. No prospect for me, perhaps. I should have seen that sooner. But why must I believe you could not be for some other? *(Pause.)* Who is she?

SHERLOCK. Please ...

VIOLET SMITH. Am I not to know my rival?

SHERLOCK. No. *(Long pause.)*

VIOLET SMITH. It's that actress, that singer ... Irene Adler.

SHERLOCK. Violet, simply because you have read Watson's rather lurid rendering of that adventure —

VIOLET SMITH. Is it she?

SHERLOCK. I cannot tell you. *(Pause.)*

VIOLET SMITH. Then tell me only this: the lady in question — is she free to marry?

SHERLOCK. *I* am not free to marry. Set your jealous mind at rest.

VIOLET SMITH. You misunderstand my reason for asking. Why are you not free to marry?

SHERLOCK. My work forbids it.

VIOLET SMITH. Other men who are serious about their work still marry.

SHERLOCK. When my uncovery of the working of the criminal mind demands the utmost in focused concentration, shall I invite distraction and confusion? In order to protect one hearth, one home, shall I sacrifice my mission to protect *all* hearths and homes? And shall I expose a wife and children to the dangers that accompany the pursuit of my calling? I tell you, I am not free to marry!

VIOLET SMITH. *(After a pause.)* Very eloquent. Yet you have a human heart. No one knows that better than I.

SHERLOCK. It is a great nuisance to me.

VIOLET SMITH. No doubt. If it did not pump the blood that fuels your machinery of deduction, you would surely have had it removed. *(He makes a gesture, somewhere between agreement and impatience.)* You think I am here merely as a jealous woman, looking to make a scene. I did not know you thought me so conventional. I am here to urge you to marry her.

SHERLOCK. What?

VIOLET SMITH. Whoever she is, whatever the circumstances you feel you cannot tell me ... that is what I urge you to do.

SHERLOCK. Indeed you are right. This is not where I thought you were leading.

VIOLET SMITH. Am I not permitted, at least, to care about you? *(Sherlock is baffled by this idea, beyond any ability to speak.)* Do you think I cannot see what effect your monastic living has upon your soul? Three years you spent abroad, looking for what was missing — you might have found it here. No, I don't mean in me. I've long since given up such thoughts. But in someone. Being an Olympian is hard to sustain. How do you do it ... when you *do* have a heart? And a chivalrous one. *(He makes a dismissive gesture.)* You can't brush this off, like an inconvenient scrap of a clue that doesn't fit the theory you're developing. You're not whole — *(Sherlock brings his fist down on a table, suddenly and unexpectedly. This shocks Violet Smith into silence momentarily. After a pause.)* Is it Irene Adler? *(He does not answer. She gathers up her things.)* I wish you well. And I wish you to know that I do not regret what has passed between us. The consequences are mine and I shall bear them proudly. Such disgrace as —

SHERLOCK. Disgrace? What possible —

VIOLET SMITH. It is no longer for you to ask.

SHERLOCK. Violet ... *(But she has turned to go, leaving Sherlock stunned and wondering. As he gradually pulls himself together, Violet Smith is restoring to Mrs. Cyril Morton. Sherlock slips away from the scene like the memory he is.)*

MRS. MORTON. So you see, Miss Sheridan ... a woman who

approaches Mr. Sherlock Holmes with a personal connection is a woman of courage.

VIOLET.   I am sorry to have so misjudged you, Mrs. Morton. But you will forgive me if I ask.... Your conversation seems to bespeak an intimacy that — You challenged him in a way that —

MRS. MORTON.   *(Quietly and firmly.)* I had the right.

VIOLET.   The disgrace to which you referred —

MRS. MORTON.   *(Interrupting.)* Was ameliorated by my marriage with Mr. Cyril Morton. It is remarkable what benefit a South African fortune can offer a young woman.

VIOLET.   But if there was a child ...

MRS. MORTON.   I lost the child.

VIOLET.   I'm sorry.

MRS. MORTON.   *I* am sorry to have to disappoint you. I wish ... *(Pause.)* Here you are, Miss Sheridan. You will be able to reach Irene Adler here. *(She gives her a piece of paper, or else writes in Violet's notebook.)*

VIOLET.   Thank you for your time. *(Mrs. Morton turns to go, then:)*

MRS. MORTON.   Miss Sheridan.... Good luck.

Scene 4

Late afternoon, toward dusk. Shadows are lengthening. A public place: a London park or open air tea house.

Violet enters warily, looking over her shoulder. We get the impression someone is following her.

Suddenly a man is standing behind her, unseen by Violet.

JACK BARTON.   Miss Sheridan? *(Violet practically jumps out of her skin. Laughing.)* Oh, pardon me. A little skittish this afternoon, I take it.

VIOLET.   I had the distinct impression that someone was following me.

JACK BARTON.   Did you? Well, don't look at me. I was escorting another lady.

VIOLET.   Is Miss Adler here?

JACK BARTON.   Gone to sniff some roses. The better to make an entrance. You know these divas.

VIOLET.   Did she suggest this meeting place so she could wander among the roses? I'm somewhat pressed for time.

JACK BARTON.   No, it was my suggestion, actually.

VIOLET.   *(Suspicious.)* I hadn't expected the added pleasure of your company, Mr. Barton.

JACK BARTON.   Oh, had you not? *(He leaves it at this. Irene appears with her arms full of flowers.)*

IRENE.   *(Breathing in the glory of nature.)* Splendid! The fragrance is celestial, Jack! Miss Sheridan, are you a lover of flowers, as I am?

VIOLET.   In their natural habitat, Miss Adler. Thank you for meeting me.

JACK BARTON.   The pleasure is ours, Miss Sheridan.

VIOLET.   Quite. I was surprised to see you outside the Carrington house.

IRENE.   *(Guarded.)* I was not surprised to see you.

VIOLET.   No?

IRENE.   No doubt your father has involved you in the case. *(Pause, as Violet digests this.)*

VIOLET.   *(Choosing her words carefully.)* What makes you think my father is involved in the case?

IRENE.   His personal interest in Lady Carrington should be enough to explain that.

VIOLET.   *(Not wanting to reveal her ignorance.)* Of course.

IRENE.   You look surprised. I don't mind mentioning it, although it was quite a source of jealousy for me at one time. I shouldn't say any more. Jack suffers from retrospective chivalry.

JACK BARTON.   *(Looking at her searchingly.)* Tell me, Miss Sheridan…. Do you trust Mr. Holmes? Do you take his words at face value?

VIOLET.   No doubt you have a good reason for asking.

IRENE.   Oh, Miss Sheridan, Jack is an actor. His profession makes him cynical.

VIOLET.   After that 'séance,' surely it is you I should mistrust. *(Barton seems more flattered than offended.)*

JACK BARTON.   You found it convincing?

VIOLET.   *(Pause.)* Rather. Yes.

IRENE.   Jack's very good, isn't he? And I, well … I'm an old trouper from way back.

VIOLET.   Quite.

IRENE.   But, my dear, you don't think we could have managed it without your father's expert help? *(Violet is stunned into silence by this. She had hung on to the hope and belief that her father was as much a 'victim' of the hoax as she.)* He has done quite a bit of research into spiritualism, just to satisfy his own curiosity. *(Pause.)*

VIOLET.   Miss Adler, obviously my father trusts you, since he enlisted your help on the little 'theatrical' the other night. I wonder whether he has enlisted your help on the Carrington case as well.

IRENE.   My help?

VIOLET.   He was always an admirer of your talents and intelligence.

IRENE.   You are too kind. But no, he has not approached me about the case.

VIOLET.   What a shame. His loss, of course. But my own inquiry can proceed more smoothly, knowing the 'state of play.'

JACK BARTON.   *(Quickly.)* And how is your inquiry going, Miss Sheridan?

VIOLET.   Very well. And yours, Mr. Barton?

JACK BARTON.   *(Taken aback.)* Mine?

VIOLET.   Yes. You were no doubt at the Carrington house for a reason when I saw you.

JACK BARTON.   Oh, that. No. Heavens, no. I'm embarrassed to say I was trying to talk Irene into commissioning a play about it. Marvellous role for her … wife of prominent politician poisons him over sherry.

VIOLET.   You're of the opinion that Lady Carrington is guilty.

JACK BARTON.   Well, of course. It's open and shut.

VIOLET.   Except —

IRENE.   Except?

VIOLET.   Except for the disguised man she saw slipping away from the house around the time of her husband's death. *(Silence.)*

JACK BARTON.   Well, your inquiry is impressive indeed. You know a great deal more about it than I. Still, there's a role in it for Irene somewhere, I'm sure.

IRENE.   Nonsense, Jack. Miss Sheridan ... I've a little inquiry of my own I'd like to pursue with you.

VIOLET.   Indeed?

IRENE.   It's of a rather personal nature.

JACK BARTON.   Just a moment, Irene. Don't look around, either of you. Miss Sheridan, I believe you were right. Someone has been following you. Keep talking, ladies, as if nothing were amiss ... *(Jack goes offstage, walking as nonchalantly as possible, to avoid suspicion.)*

IRENE.   Goodness. Suddenly I'm too shy to know how to proceed.

VIOLET.   I think I may be able to guess the subject.

IRENE.   *(Looking at her deeply.)* Yes. No doubt you can. *(Pause.)* I told Mr. Holmes — your father — it was unfair to play with your desire to know.

VIOLET.   And?

IRENE.   He said he has his reasons. He is not an easy man to argue with.

VIOLET.   No. So you went along.

IRENE.   I wanted to meet you. To see you, at least. It was one way to do so. I've felt so — *(Irene stops herself.)*

VIOLET.   *(Eager.)* So...?

IRENE.   No, I mustn't. I promised your father I wouldn't say anything.

VIOLET.   You wanted to meet me —

IRENE.   *(Quickly.)* Curiosity. Is that so surprising?

VIOLET.   It depends.

IRENE.   I knew your father rather well.... At one time. *(Pause.)* What are you thinking?

VIOLET.   You may have answered a question for me. 'Curiosity' seems a passionless emotion —

IRENE.   Do you think so? You, whose heart beats with the blood of Sherlock Holmes? Curiosity — passionless? *(From off-stage there is a commotion that doesn't quite count as a scuffle — just a bit of physical awkwardness, maybe some ad-libs. Jack Barton returns escorting [more or less by the scruff of the neck] a rather abashed Charles.)*

JACK BARTON.   *(In an Irish accent.)* Well, if it isn't our young friend from the séance? Surely he'd be more comfortable joining us than lurking about in the undergrowth ... *(Charles is embarrassed enough to be caught, but when he catches sight of Irene Adler he stops dead still, astounded.)* Come along, my friend. You look as though you've just seen a ghost.

IRENE.   *(Laughing with Jack.)* He has, Jack. Now, be kind. *(Charles may be permitted a double-take, or perhaps a triple, between Irene, alive, and Jack, whom he met as Turlough ... and Violet sitting amongst them as cool as can be.)*

JACK BARTON.   Your bodyguard has a few things to learn about camouflage and disguise, Miss Sheridan.

VIOLET.   If Mr. Yorke is serving as my bodyguard, Mr. Barton, it is strictly on a volunteer basis.

JACK BARTON.   Well, he looks like an able and willing volunteer. I'd train him up, if I were you. Could be handy in a tight spot.

VIOLET.   I hardly think so.

CHARLES.   Violet, I —

VIOLET.   Charles Wellington Yorke, allow me to introduce Miss Irene Adler. And Mr. John Barton, late of the Lyceum.

CHARLES.   Oh, I say. An actor.

VIOLET.   Ably deduced.

IRENE.   Won't you join us, Mr. Yorke?

VIOLET.   I'm sure Mr. Yorke has other more pressing business.

CHARLES.   Well, no, actually —

JACK BARTON.   *(Teasing; in his Irish accent.)* Pull up a piece of turf there, young thing.

IRENE.   Now, Jack, behave yourself!

CHARLES.   *(Sotto voce, to Violet.)* I have some information for you.

VIOLET.   *(Sotto voce.)* Not interested.

CHARLES.   *(Sotto voce.)* It's as much as my life is worth to have it.

JACK BARTON.   Would it be about the Carrington case, then? *(Charles turns suddenly to stare at him — partly surprised that Barton knows, partly mortified that his sotto voce obviously wasn't sotto enough.)*

CHARLES.   Well, um ...

JACK BARTON.   Don't worry. We've been chatting up a storm about it with Miss Sheridan here.

IRENE.   Yes, it's most intriguing! What is your new information? *(Pause.)*

JACK BARTON.   Your caution is commendable, Mr. Yorke. But you're among friends here. As Miss Sheridan will tell you. *(Irish accent again.)* Won't you, Miss? Your young friend obviously thinks we pulled his leg the other evening all on our own hook.

VIOLET.   We must congratulate Mr. Barton as well as Miss Adler on the effectiveness of their 'séance.' We were quite taken in, weren't we, Charles?

CHARLES.   Oh, yes. Smashingly done. *(Jack and Irene bow their heads ever so modestly.)*

VIOLET.   And being the generous artists they are, they do, of course, give credit to my father's coaching. *(Charles simply stares at Violet — a look which is not lost on Jack or Irene. He recovers himself as quickly as he can.)*

CHARLES.   The old boy's a clever one, isn't he?

IRENE.   *(Significantly.)* I've long been an admirer of his theatrical abilities. And his talent for setting up a scenario to suit his needs.

JACK BARTON.   From a couple of professionals — you know that compliment is worth something. *(Suddenly all bluff and hearty.)* Now, where can you have gotten new information from? Scotland Yard has no clues whatever. Or so it says in the papers.

CHARLES. *(Sotto voce to Violet.)* Friend of my father's. A Cabinet Minister. Knows — That is to say, knew Lord Carrington. One of two or three people who was close to him. He was over at the house last night. I overheard them discussing Lord Carrington's death. They've found a substance in his bloodstream — a poison that's hard to identify. Not known in Europe. A natural venom of some kind. They're working on it. But it's very hush-hush. Practically the only clue they've got. *(Violet takes this in. Jack, who has been attempting to eavesdrop, looks at Irene.)*

JACK BARTON. Well, if this is all hush-hush, we shouldn't be intruding. Shall we go, Irene?

IRENE. Certainly. *(Rises; then stops to look at Violet.)* Did you know there were Sheridans in my husband's family?

VIOLET. I didn't.

IRENE. Of course not. How could you know? Goodbye, my dear.

VIOLET. Goodbye.

JACK BARTON. *(As a parting line.)* You know, I learned a bit about venoms in a play I did once.

VIOLET. Did you?

JACK BARTON. Apparently you can make a quite deadly little number from the venom of bees. *(He looks significantly at Violet.)*

VIOLET. What on earth would make you think of that?

JACK BARTON. Oh, just your mention of a disguised man slipping away from the house. I suppose that was in the play too. We really must be off, mustn't we, Irene? *(Irene nods regally to Violet and Charles, as Barton ushers her away. Charles and Violet are left alone together.)*

VIOLET. He thinks my father's implicated.

CHARLES. What?

VIOLET. Bee venom. A disguised man.

CHARLES. That's preposterous!

VIOLET. Well, you're the one who came dropping out of

the heavens, or rather bursting out of the bushes, bearing clues for me, thank you very much.

CHARLES.   But it's inconceivable that your father —

VIOLET.   They both told me in their way not to trust him. That bogus séance ...

CHARLES.   You're right there. Your father does turn out to be a bit of a shammer after all.

VIOLET.   Why couldn't he take on the case himself? And it seems he has some kind of personal interest in Lady Carrington. Charles, you don't think my father capable of a crime of passion...?

CHARLES.   No. *(Pause.)* Well, he has a passionate *mind.* But after all these years it would be more a crime of dotage — no offence.

VIOLET.   Three different women ...

CHARLES.   Oh, yes, I see your point, but still ...

VIOLET.   He's a dark horse. And it's *not* impossible.

CHARLES.   What shall we do?

VIOLET.   We?

CHARLES.   You don't think I could let you face this alone —

VIOLET.   Charles ...

CHARLES.   No, really, darling. I've been thinking —

VIOLET.   A dangerous occupation for a gentleman.

CHARLES.   *(Not to be daunted.)* It's more what I *feel.* I've learned that what I feel is more important than — *(Violet makes an impatient gesture worthy of her father. Charles almost allows discouragement to overtake him, then rallies.)* Well, don't you need a — a Watson? *(Violet laughs.)* Friends? *(A moment.)*

VIOLET.   Friends. *(Shifting gears.)* I must go and see him.

CHARLES.   I'll come with you.

VIOLET.   No. You find out more about this poison business.

CHARLES.   All right. *(As she goes.)* Violet. It seems we're both on the trail of venomous creatures.

VIOLET.   I'm afraid you may be right.

Scene 5

The next day. Sussex. The drone of bees fills the air. Sherlock, wrapped in a blanket, dozes at the table. Again, lights and sound distort and we are inside his dream.

WOMAN. *(Voice over.)* Are we decided, then?
SHERLOCK. *(Voice over.)* I see no alternative. Do you?
WOMAN. *(Voice over.)* Surely ...
SHERLOCK. *(Voice over.)* We've been through this, over and over.
WOMAN. *(Voice over.)* I only wish —
SHERLOCK. *(Voice over.)* We can't indulge in wishes. We must live in reality.
WOMAN. *(Voice over.)* Let's be quick then. *(The sound of a baby crying slowly transmutes into ... Violet gently calling "Father ... father ... Mr. Holmes." Violet is standing at the head of the garden path. Suddenly afraid, she comes over and touches his shoulder and Sherlock wakes, startling them both. Violet is unsettled to see him looking frail.)*
SHERLOCK. Ahh, there you are.
VIOLET. Are you all right?
SHERLOCK. As you see.
VIOLET. But what's the matter? *(Sherlock waves his hand dismissively. Violet joins him.)*
SHERLOCK. Well, what have you found out?
VIOLET. A great deal.
SHERLOCK. Good.
VIOLET. You won't like much of it.
SHERLOCK. I had no expectations of liking the information.
VIOLET. Just as well. *(Brief pause.)*
SHERLOCK. Well?
VIOLET. Let's start with the séance hoax you treated us to the other night.
SHERLOCK. Ahh.

VIOLET.   Have you nothing to say about that?

SHERLOCK.   I told you: You were off on the wrong trail.

VIOLET.   So you had to throw me off the scent.

SHERLOCK.   If you like. How did you fare with Lady Carrington?

VIOLET.   As well as can be expected.

SHERLOCK.   How did she account for the events on the afternoon of her husband's death?

VIOLET.   She would not.

SHERLOCK.   *(With consternation.)* Did you tell her who you are?

VIOLET.   Not right away.

SHERLOCK.   *(Flaring.)* But I told you —

VIOLET.   I wanted to make my way independently of our — family connection. *(Sherlock rolls his eyes as if this were simply beyond the pale.)*

SHERLOCK.   And what was her response when you finally deigned to do as I had instructed you?

VIOLET.   She became very angry.

SHERLOCK.   Oh?

VIOLET.   And she told me that she had been blackmailed once before, as a young woman.

SHERLOCK.   *(Cautiously.)* Yes?

VIOLET.   Extraordinary.

SHERLOCK.   What is?

VIOLET.   That someone should experience two unrelated incidents of blackmail in the course of her life.

SHERLOCK.   Did she tell you anything else?

VIOLET.   Yes, in fact. She was not with her husband at five o'clock, but rather returned home shortly before six.

SHERLOCK.   *(Underwhelmed.)* Yes?

VIOLET.   And as she approached the house, observed a figure stealing away through the French windows. A tall man, solidly built, dark hair, wearing a handlebar moustache so large it struck her as being a false one.

SHERLOCK.   *(Guarded.)* You mean, like part of a disguise?

VIOLET.   Precisely.

SHERLOCK. This is very little to go on.

VIOLET. And what of her relationship with you?

SHERLOCK. *(Wary.)* I beg your pardon?

VIOLET. Three different women seem to have had relationships with you. Serious relationships.

SHERLOCK. That is a matter of perspective. *(Sherlock merely raises his eyebrows and waits for her to elaborate.)*

VIOLET. Lady Carrington. Mrs. Cyril Morton, who used to be Violet Smith. Irene Adler. *(Holmes makes a dismissive gesture.)* What do you mean by that gesture? Are you denying what I say?

SHERLOCK. *(After a pause.)* Your investigative skills are more impressive than I expected.

VIOLET. And yet a mystery remains. As far as I can tell, any one of those women might be my mother.

SHERLOCK. Perhaps.

VIOLET. Who is it?

SHERLOCK. I told you ... I will not tell you.

VIOLET. Does none of them mean anything to you?

SHERLOCK. That question is off limits.

VIOLET. Do *I* mean nothing to you? *(Suddenly and without warning, Holmes sweeps a bunch of papers off the table. But this exertion gives way to a fit of coughing, from which it takes him a moment to recover.)*

SHERLOCK. Damn it! This has nothing to do with the issue at hand.

VIOLET. *(After a pause.)* Does it not?

SHERLOCK. I sent you to investigate a murder and you return with nothing but rumours from love-sick females mooning over romantic memories.

VIOLET. What I have learned is relevant to the Carrington case.

SHERLOCK. Is it indeed?

VIOLET. At this moment, you are the clearest suspect. *(Holmes stops in his tracks, thunderstruck. Then he lets out a derisive laugh.)*

SHERLOCK. What makes me so?

VIOLET. Your relationship with Lady Carrington, which gives you a motive. And the toxins found in Lord Carrington's body, derived from a natural source — a natural venom, very possibly a species of bee. And a man in disguise slipping away from the house shortly before Lord Carrington was found dead. *(Pause.)*

SHERLOCK. I see.

VIOLET. Why should you be any less capable of committing a crime for love than another man? You pretend to be free of human attachments. It is an excellent cover.

SHERLOCK. It is not a cover. "Human attachments," as you call them ... God, it sounds positively ghoulish.

VIOLET. *(Ignoring the joke.)* They are necessary to everyone.

SHERLOCK. *Not* to me. I have made a study of the human heart, in all its depravity. I have seen the most horrible crimes arise from the tenderest motives. I have seen what kind of behaviour "human attachments" inspire.

VIOLET. Then you are worse than I thought.

SHERLOCK. You thought me capable of murder. Now you think me worse than that?

VIOLET. Yes.

SHERLOCK. An extraordinary statement.

VIOLET. You are cold —

SHERLOCK. But I am *sharp*. And my sharpness serves a purp — *(Suddenly he lapses into a fit of coughing. They both become aware that his sharpness is tempered by exceptional frailty at this moment. As he recovers himself he checks the handkerchief.)* Any mediocre soul can plod his way through life with a wife and a brood of children. What does he leave behind him but more potential victims for the criminal mind to exploit?

VIOLET. But if you care for humanity so much, how can you deny your own?

SHERLOCK. In order for humanity to thrive, not all of us can be merely human. Some of us must sacrifice the common pleasures and pursuits. It is the price.

VIOLET. But you do not pay it alone. It is paid by all who are close to you.

SHERLOCK.   So be it.

VIOLET.   Three different women were given to believe in a vision of happiness with you —

SHERLOCK.   Three grown women. Perfectly capable of handling their visions — or hallucinations — of happiness.

VIOLET.   Three grown women. And one baby — crying alone in a Swiss nursery. Crying for what seems like hours. Finally a light goes on in the hall. There's a silhouette in the doorway. Tell me — if that silhouette had been yours, would it really have diminished your greatness? If the voice that said "Ssh now" had been yours, or my own mother's, do you really think the world would be less safe for decent people to live in? If, instead of a stranger's hand patting my covers and turning out the light again, a familiar hand had held mine for just a few moments while I fell asleep again — would your system of deduction suddenly have shown a flaw? You might have had your heir legitimately, and raised her too. *(Pause.)*

SHERLOCK.   At that time I was not looking for an heir.

VIOLET.   No, I was just one of your wild oats that had the temerity to sprout. And now you want to cultivate me, for your own purposes.

SHERLOCK.   Violet. You're not being fair.

VIOLET.   Am I not?

SHERLOCK.   You're young. You haven't yet looked mortality in the face. The world looks different under its gaze. *(This slows her down but doesn't stop her.)*

VIOLET.   What view of mortality are you looking at? Through the hangman's noose? *(This stops him. For a long moment.)*

SHERLOCK.   Violet, you must believe me. I was not present when Lord Carrington died.

VIOLET.   *(Taking out her notebook.)* And have you any witnesses?

SHERLOCK.   Yes. Lady Carrington. *(Violet is stopped in her tracks.)* When she arrived home and found her husband dead, she was returning from being with me. *(Pause.)* Violet, I need your help.

Scene 6

Violet's studio. Charles waits for her. Violet arrives in a bit of a hurry.

CHARLES.   Ahh, there you are. What did the old boy have to say?

VIOLET.   A great deal.

CHARLES.   I've been pursuing the bee research —

VIOLET.   Charles.... He was with Lady Carrington before she returned home that day. They are one another's alibi.

CHARLES.   I say. You thought there was something between them ... I suppose you were right.

VIOLET.   She was appealing to him for help because she was being blackmailed.

CHARLES.   *(A light glimmering in the back of his mind.)* Then she returned home and found her husband dead?

VIOLET.   That's what we don't know. She won't offer any details about what happened on her return to the house.

CHARLES.   Well, perhaps she's ready to talk now.

VIOLET.   How's that?

CHARLES.   This arrived while you were out. *(He hands her a note in an envelope, addressed to her. Violet opens it — and discovers that the envelope has already been opened.)*

VIOLET.   Charles! It's open.

CHARLES.   Sorry. *(Reciting.)* "Miss Sheridan, please come to the house at midnight tonight. I have information for you. Be sure to enter through the garden and come to the French doors. Come alone. Charlotte Carrington." *(Violet holds the paper up to the light and examines the watermark.)* I'll come with you, of course.

VIOLET.   *(Hesitating for a brief moment.)* No. She says to come alone.

CHARLES.   But Violet — midnight!

VIOLET.   Charles, no argument. Let me just think what I

have to take. There isn't much time. *(As she prepares.)*

CHARLES. What about that poison, then?

VIOLET. My father says Lord Carrington served in India for quite a few years. He might have had access to any number of exotic substances.

CHARLES. What, just lying about the house?

VIOLET. No, not exactly.

CHARLES. Poisoned by a substance in his own possession? That doesn't look good for Lady Carrington, does it?

VIOLET. When the impossible has been eliminated, whatever remains —

CHARLES. However improbable, must be the truth.

VIOLET. Well, I'm off.

CHARLES. Are you sure I can't —

VIOLET. Very sure. *Please* wait for me here. I need to know the home fires are burning.

CHARLES. *(Unhappily.)* Very well. Be careful. *(Violet goes. Charles is left for a moment — then he sits down and pulls a gun out from where it has been hidden. He starts to load it. He doesn't notice that the note from Lady Carrington has dropped to the ground. Footsteps outside. Sherlock enters, looking like a man who really shouldn't be out of bed. Charles is caught, and has no alternative but to let Sherlock see the gun.)*

SHERLOCK. I need to see Violet.

CHARLES. She's not here.

SHERLOCK. Where has she gone?

CHARLES. Out.

SHERLOCK. Leaving you to guard the sculpture? *(Charles is stung into momentary silence. Sherlock sees the note on the floor and moves down on it before Charles can prevent him. Sherlock reads the note, then holds it up to the light to check the watermark.)*

CHARLES. *(Trying to recover his dignity.)* I didn't know the trains from Sussex ran so late.

SHERLOCK. If you don't get out of London a bit you don't get to know much. Has she gone to the Carrington house?

CHARLES. Yes.

SHERLOCK. By herself?

CHARLES. I am not planning to let her be there alone.

SHERLOCK. *(Eyeing the gun.)* Just as well. This note is not from Lady Carrington.

CHARLES. What's that?

SHERLOCK. *(Hesitatingly.)* I know her hand. She did not write this.

CHARLES. Damn it!

SHERLOCK. Indeed. So you have let her set out on her own.

CHARLES. *(Bristling.)* As she wished it. And I will not hear from *you*, of all people, about the need to protect Violet. If it weren't for you, she wouldn't be exposing herself to danger this way.

SHERLOCK. What do you mean?

CHARLES. Lady Carrington wouldn't talk to you about what happened when she returned home. We don't even know whether her husband was alive or dead when she got there. But we do know that she had a relationship with you. What if her husband knew as well?

SHERLOCK. Who would tell him?

CHARLES. Lady Carrington.

SHERLOCK. *(Smiling wryly.)* Clearly you don't know the lady.

CHARLES. Maybe not. But if you ask me, her husband knew, and she's protecting you from finding that out.

SHERLOCK. If her husband knew then the blackmailer had played his hand. What time is it?

CHARLES. Quarter past eleven.

SHERLOCK. We've no time to lose.

CHARLES. You stay here — you're not well enough to go!

SHERLOCK. I *must* go.

CHARLES. Damn it, you'll only slow me down! *(Charles physically restrains him, a little too roughly. They are both momentarily shocked.)* I'm sorry, sir. I didn't mean anything by it. But I think I should go alone. I'm armed. Don't worry, Violet will be safe.

SHERLOCK. *(Hesitantly.)* Very well. You'll let me know as soon as all is clear.

CHARLES. Of course, sir. *(Charles holds out his hand and Sherlock somewhat reluctantly shakes it. Then Charles turns to go.*

Sherlock sits for a while, seeming drained of strength, but a bit pleased at the gumption Charles has just displayed. Once he's sure Charles has a good head start, he gathers himself together, and heads for the door.)

Scene 7

The grounds of the Carrington house. As Violet approaches we hear her thoughts in voice over.

SHERLOCK. *(Voice over.)* Are you sure?

LADY CARRINGTON. *(Voice over.)* There's no question. Blackmail.

SHERLOCK. *(Voice over.)* Damn!

LADY CARRINGTON. *(Voice over.)* You've got to help me.

SHERLOCK. *(Voice over.)* I'll lay plans in my own way.

IRENE. *(Voice over.)* But, my dear, you don't think we could have managed it without your father's expert help —

MRS. MORTON. *(Voice over.)* You remind me of myself ... when I was your age.

LADY CARRINGTON. *(Voice over.)* No question. Blackmail.

SHERLOCK. *(Voice over.)* In my own way —

IRENE. *(Voice over.)* What seems intimate to one, another experiences as distance.

LADY CARRINGTON. *(Voice over.)* You've got to help me.

SHERLOCK. *(Voice over.)* In my own way. It may take time ...

VIOLET SMITH. *(Voice over.)* Am I not to know my rival? *(Violet moves through the shadows toward the French windows of the house. Quietly and with some expertise, she breaks in. As she moves through the darkness of the room, we see that a figure is sitting, brooding. It is Lady Carrington.)*

LADY CARRINGTON. Who's there? *(Violet shines her flashlight on her own face.)* It's you! *(Recovering herself.)* What are you doing here?

VIOLET. You sent for me.

LADY CARRINGTON. I?

VIOLET.   It was urgent.

LADY CARRINGTON.   I sent nothing.

VIOLET.   Then, Lady Carrington, someone *else* has summoned me here. And no doubt that someone else will keep his rendezvous. We've only half an hour.

LADY CARRINGTON.   *(Sinking into a chair.)* God help us.

VIOLET.   We are quite capable of helping ourselves, Lady Carrington, if you will only shed some light on who this person might be.

LADY CARRINGTON.   Very well.

VIOLET.   *(As Lady Carrington hesitates.)* Let me help you. I know that you were being blackmailed. With what?

LADY CARRINGTON.   The man has ... a document.

VIOLET.   A document? One you did not wish your husband to see.

LADY CARRINGTON.   That is correct.

VIOLET.   And this man still has the document in his possession?

LADY CARRINGTON.   I presume so.

VIOLET.   Good. Why would you not tell my father what happened when you arrived home and found your husband dead?

LADY CARRINGTON.   I did not find my husband dead.

VIOLET.   What's that?

LADY CARRINGTON.   He was still alive. Or barely.

VIOLET.   You spoke?

LADY CARRINGTON.   Yes.

VIOLET.   What about?

LADY CARRINGTON.   Things in our past. *(She hesitates again.)*

VIOLET.   Lady Carrington, we haven't much time.

LADY CARRINGTON.   *(With resolve.)* No one knows the particulars I am about to divulge to you. I trust it will remain that way.

VIOLET.   Of course.

LADY CARRINGTON.   I should say, no one but myself and Mr. Holmes.

VIOLET.   I see.

LADY CARRINGTON.   We met during the case which was chronicled by Dr. Watson as "The Adventure of Charles

Augustus Milverton."

VIOLET. *(Stirred.)* There was a lady in that case ... unnamed, married to a peer of the realm. A victim of Milverton's blackmail; she shot him in cold blood. And Holmes allowed her to escape.

LADY CARRINGTON. I was not married to Lord Carrington at the time, although your supposition is understandable. But I was a victim of Mr. Milverton's blackmail, as I told you. And the lady who shot Charles Augustus Milverton was my friend.

VIOLET. I have read the case since last we met. Milverton made a close study of young ladies in society of marriageable age ... watched for matches broken off.

LADY CARRINGTON. Exactly. I learned that a close friend, already married to a prominent man, had faced the same fate as I.

VIOLET. Yes, that's in the story! Milverton had made good his threat ... revealed a secret to her husband that broke his heart and led him to his deathbed.

LADY CARRINGTON. She came to me and confided her desperate resolve: to kill Charles Augustus Milverton. She had less to lose than I, and I felt I had little enough.

I proposed to her a dangerous scheme. Living in my father's house was torment, especially as I felt Milverton's trap closing around me. I had already planned to run away. Now I knew where to go. I would disguise myself and find a position in Milverton's own house — and once inside, I could open the way for my friend to come safely one night with her revolver and end the mad dog's life. My own fate I cared little for — it was sealed in a safe in his house. So one night I stole away from my father's home. With my friend's help I obtained the clothing and accent of a respectable working class girl, and I applied for a position in Milverton's home in the person of —

VIOLET. *(Wide-eyed.)* Agatha.

LADY CARRINGTON. Yes. I see you have read Dr. Watson's account closely.

VIOLET. That was not what made me think of it.

LADY CARRINGTON. No? Well, as you have guessed, I became employed there as 'Agatha' and learned the ways of the household. As I watched for opportunities to pave the way for my friend, a tradesman came to the house making inquiries.

VIOLET.   Sherlock Holmes.

LADY CARRINGTON.   Yes. He singled me out and befriended me. I was the newest in the household but perhaps I also seemed the most open. And I was intrigued by him. I watched my own behaviour carefully, always fearful that I might betray myself by a wrong word or gesture. And in my vigilance, I noticed that every now and then this tradesman would betray himself with a wrong word or gesture. No one else noticed, I'm sure. But when I confronted him on a few mistakes, he looked deeply at me — I would almost say into me — and I felt my own disguise being penetrated. It was only natural that we should reveal ourselves to one another ... although haltingly and fearfully at first. He was a man not accustomed to being seen through. And it seems that once he had let me peek, he couldn't stop. The feeling seemed to draw him, although he fought it. I looked deeper into him, and he into me. Soon we put it about that we were engaged, to explain the inordinate amounts of time we chose to spend together.

When he learned of my plight and my friend's plan, our pact was sealed. He was there to stop Milverton himself, but becoming involved with ... an individual who was experiencing pain at this man's hands, only sharpened his resolve. I would help *him* to enter the monster's lair. And he swore to me that he would crack the safe and destroy the papers that compromised me and every other lady within Milverton's power.

VIOLET.   Very chivalrous.

LADY CARRINGTON.   Oh, yes. It was certainly that. And in my case it was something more. It was a declaration of —

VIOLET.   Of love?

LADY CARRINGTON.   *(Feeling she has revealed too much.)* Perhaps I should not place words in Mr. Holmes's mouth.

VIOLET.   When you returned home the day of your husband's death ... you had been with my father. *(Pause.)*

LADY CARRINGTON.   When I came home on that ... terrible day ... I found my husband barely conscious. I was late, as I have told you. With what strength he had left, my husband asked me whether I had just been with Mr. Holmes. I was astonished. I could not imagine how he might have guessed. But he charged me on my life to tell the truth — and so I did. He was a man whose heart knew little of forgiveness. And as he breathed his last ... *(For a moment, she cannot speak.)*

VIOLET. *(Gently.)* Go on, Lady Carrington. I know how difficult this is.

LADY CARRINGTON. With his last breath he said, "You have murdered me." *(Pause.)*

VIOLET. And the man you saw stealing away from the house before you returned.... You think he told your husband of your relations with Mr. Holmes?

LADY CARRINGTON. I cannot think how else he knew. And yet I cannot think how *anyone* could have known. I thought perhaps this stranger had murdered my husband. And yet his last words to me ...

JACK BARTON. Were true. In their way. *(Violet and Lady Carrington whirl around, startled, to find Jack Barton pointing a gun at them.)* An absorbing story, Lady Carrington. Thank you for distracting Miss Sheridan for me.

VIOLET. Mr. Barton.

LADY CARRINGTON. You know this man?

VIOLET. Yes. And you have seen him too, Lady Carrington. Although no doubt you fail to recognize him without his hugely over-sized moustache. The one you thought looked false. Tell me, Barton, did Lord Carrington laugh in your face before you killed him?

JACK BARTON. *(Sharply.)* I didn't kill him, Miss Sheridan. You heard the lady. She did.

LADY CARRINGTON. What are you saying? I don't understand.

JACK BARTON. I merely visited Lord Carrington to discuss a small matter of business.

VIOLET. There is a name for that kind of business.

JACK BARTON. Save it. I expected that Lady Carrington's

doings would be of great interest to her husband.

VIOLET.   And did you come away with a large sum of money?

JACK BARTON.   I did not. I came away a murder suspect. Shall we say, I underestimated the man I was dealing with.

VIOLET.   He faced you down.

JACK BARTON.   He did more than that. He told me frankly he would not accede to my demands. And then he pulled a snuff box from an inside pocket. Instead of popping open the lid, he slid open a panel at the bottom of the box, and took out a curious-looking pellet. As cool as a cucumber, he said, "You will regret this folly till the end of your days." And then he said (Lady Carrington will recognize this line), "You have murdered me." He swallowed the pellet, washing it down with sherry from his glass.

LADY CARRINGTON.   My God.

VIOLET.   And then?

JACK BARTON.   And then? How should I know, Miss Sheridan? My feet had already carried me halfway to the garden wall before I knew where I was. I was looking for a little money — I found a lot of trouble.

VIOLET.   You had got nowhere blackmailing Lady Carrington, so you decided to go directly to her husband. It's a good story, Mr. Barton, but you have no witnesses.

JACK BARTON.   Exactly. Or rather, I *had* no witnesses. Until the story got out about a man seen leaving the Carrington house around the time of the death.

VIOLET.   And now you find yourself, I suppose, obliged to leave the country.

JACK BARTON.   It would be ... convenient.

VIOLET.   An excellent idea. Why don't you go? We won't report you to the authorities.

JACK BARTON.   It wouldn't matter if you did. My profession has equipped me to pass unrecognized where I wish to go.

VIOLET.   But one problem remains. You still need money — and that's why you're here.

JACK BARTON.   Very good, Miss Sheridan. And I also need you off my trail. That's why *you're* here. And I need your assurance that Mr. Sherlock Holmes will not plague me. You can protect me ... I believe he will listen to you. And now, Lady Carrington —

LADY CARRINGTON.   If my husband would not yield to your demands, what makes you think that I will?

VIOLET.   Don't be silly, Lady Carrington. Pay the man. You've got the money.

LADY CARRINGTON.   But —

VIOLET.   He's got a gun and I have no doubt he knows how to use it. Never barter with a man who has nothing to lose. He's in this deep, why should he stop at murder?

JACK BARTON.   Quite right, Miss. Lady Carrington, if I must play the desperado, you have your husband to thank.

LADY CARRINGTON.   I'll have to go —

VIOLET.   *(Quickly.)* There's your handbag right there, Lady Carrington. I'm sure the pocket money you carry with you will be enough to get Mr. Barton safely to the Continent.

LADY CARRINGTON.   *('Getting' it.)* Yes, of course. No point in being coy. Now, I've left my reading glasses ...

VIOLET.   For God's sake, please just give me your handbag.

LADY CARRINGTON.   *(Doing so.)* Mister ... Barton, is it? You have won the day. Need you point that thing quite so directly at me? *(Barton lowers his gun slightly. Violet draws hers from the handbag, which is actually her own, and points it at him.)*

VIOLET.   Lower it all the way to the floor, Barton. *(After he does so.)* You men always make the mistake of thinking every woman's handbag looks the same. *(Violet nods to Lady Carrington, who moves in to pick up Barton's gun and put it away somewhere safe.)* It makes me feel better about you, Barton, to know that although you may be a professional actor, when it comes to being a crook you're the rankest amateur.

JACK BARTON.   *(Wryly.)* Thank you, Miss Sheridan. *(Charles has slipped in through the French doors and is aiming his own gun at Barton.)*

CHARLES.   Don't make a move, Barton.

VIOLET.   He's not likely to, Charles. We've disarmed him.

CHARLES.   Violet, thank God you're safe! You'd no idea what

79

danger you were in. Mr. Holmes to' ' me that note wasn't from Lady Carrington!

VIOLET.   I know, Charles.

JACK BARTON.   How?

VIOLET.   The watermark. You see what I mean about amateurism, Mr. Barton. Surely you don't imagine a woman of Lady Carrington's position would use paper made by a middle grade London stationer.

CHARLES.   Oh, I say!

VIOLET.   I know the firm. They make rather a good sketch paper as well.

SHERLOCK.   Well done. *(Sherlock has entered the room unobserved.)* Anticipation is the greatest weapon in outwitting the criminal mind. Obviously you were ready for Mr. Barton.

CHARLES.   Mr. Holmes! *(To Violet.)* I *told* him —

SHERLOCK.   Told me what, young man?

CHARLES.   *(To Violet.)* He's not well.

SHERLOCK.   *(To Violet.)* What do you plan to do with your prisoner?

CHARLES.   Well, he's got to be turned in, hasn't he? He's a murderer.

SHERLOCK.   Not quite. Unless you count driving a man to suicide ...

VIOLET.   How did you know?

SHERLOCK.   No trace of poison in the glass or the decanter.

CHARLES.   But still —

SHERLOCK.   Yes, Charles, you're right. But still. Mr. Barton has done quite enough to warrant the full fury of the law.

VIOLET.   Just a moment. Mr. Barton still possesses a document of rather particular interest to me. A souvenir of a trip to Switzerland with Irene Adler. She was your tour guide to a number of small churches.

JACK BARTON.   Why would Miss Adler take me on a tour of Swiss churches?

VIOLET.   Curiosity. Passionate curiosity, fuelled by jealousy. And when she found the information she sought, you filched the documentary evidence. And brought it with you to England where you suspected it could be very profitable for you. *(Pause.)* I'd like to see it. *(Barton hesitates.)*

SHERLOCK. Don't be a fool, man. Who will buy it from you now? It's over. *(Barton pulls a paper from his pocket and hands it over to Violet. Violet takes it almost gingerly, then looks at the paper long and hard.)*

VIOLET. *(To Holmes.)* I'm surprised you signed your own name.

SHERLOCK. We were obliged to show our papers. *(Violet is looking at Sherlock. Charles is watching Violet. Barton seizes his moment and flings himself at Charles. Sherlock sees the move and gets up to go after him. Charles and Barton struggle. Violet tries to get a clear shot. In the melee, a gun goes off, reverberating through the darkness. Our eyes are drawn by Sherlock collapsing and Lady Carrington running to him — so we do not see that Barton too has collapsed.)*

LADY CARRINGTON. Come quickly!

VIOLET. Charles! My father! *(Charles runs to see. Together he and Lady Carrington help Sherlock into a chair.)*

CHARLES. He's not hit.

VIOLET. But Barton is. *(We see that Barton is clutching his leg in great pain. Violet, covering him with her gun, moves closer to see. Charles comes down to her, leaving Sherlock in the care of Lady Carrington.)*

CHARLES. Your father will be all right. Sheer exhaustion.

VIOLET. We'd better get Barton some help.

CHARLES. Where?

SHERLOCK. Scotland Yard. *(Violet turns to look at him.)*

VIOLET. If we turn him in, the whole story is bound to come out. *(Sherlock looks at Lady Carrington. Then both look back to Violet, who waits.)*

SHERLOCK. You heard me, Charles. Would you be kind enough to escort Mr. Barton into the hands of the authorities.

CHARLES. Right, sir. *(Charles, with a look to Violet, helps Barton up.)*

JACK BARTON. *(To Holmes.)* I want you to know that Irene had no idea —

81

SHERLOCK.   Just get out. *(Charles escorts Barton out. In the melee, the birth document has fallen to the floor. Lady Carrington leaves Holmes's side to retrieve the document and bring it down to Violet.)*

LADY CARRINGTON.   Violet. I believe this should belong to you.

VIOLET.   *(Shaking her head.)* I don't need it — mother. I know who I am. *(Lady Carrington keeps the document. Perhaps she takes Violet's hand, touches her cheek or embraces her — some non-verbal moment between the women is needed. Then:)* Will he be all right?

SHERLOCK.   *(Behind them.)* He'll be fine. *(Violet goes up to Sherlock. He looks up at her quite tenderly. She looks closely at him.)*

VIOLET.   How could you?

SHERLOCK.   What?

VIOLET.   How could you make me track my own mother like a bloodhound. Allow me to meet her without knowing who she was. Why did you conceal the truth from me?

SHERLOCK.   Your mother needed my help. I needed your help. If you had known who she was you would have become too emotionally involved. I needed you clear-headed.

VIOLET.   And why use Barton in that bogus séance if you knew he was —

SHERLOCK.   I wanted you to meet him. Or rather him to meet you.

VIOLET.   I don't understand.

SHERLOCK.   I thought perhaps if he knew who you were he would approach you with the papers —

VIOLET.   And thus play his hand.

SHERLOCK.   Precisely.

VIOLET.   By threatening to ruin my marriage plans.

SHERLOCK.   Well, you managed that for yourself.

VIOLET.   I had some help from you in that regard.

SHERLOCK.   Not my intention ... exactly.

VIOLET.   *(To Holmes.)* So what you're saying is that you used me to bait a trap for Barton, and your plan backfired.

SHERLOCK.   Well ...

VIOLET.   And since you had refused to tell — Lady Carrington ... what you were doing to try to help her, she gave up hope and refused to speak to you.
SHERLOCK.   Things moved more slowly than I had expected.
VIOLET.   And you sent me to her, thinking that would provoke her to speak.
LADY CARRINGTON.   Of all the manipulative —
SHERLOCK.   Charlotte, I was desperate. It just wasn't working the way I'd planned. Suddenly I was afraid I'd — bungled it. Had put you and Violet in danger. That I'd ...
VIOLET.   Lost your touch? *(He says nothing. He moves to one side and thinks, as the women watch him. Finally he speaks.)*
SHERLOCK.   You came here knowing that your mother was in danger. You have accomplished what I set out to do. *(Violet bows her head, suddenly ashamed at how far she has pushed him.)*
VIOLET.   *(With difficulty.)* No ... father. *We* accomplished what you set out to do. And I've learned a great deal from you.
SHERLOCK.   Good. *(Pause.)* You still have a good deal more to learn.
VIOLET.   Do I?
SHERLOCK.   Yes. *(A little afraid of rejection.)* I'm tired now, Violet. Why don't you call on me tomorrow afternoon. I could offer you a few pointers.
VIOLET.   I see.
SHERLOCK.   Unless you feel there are no more mysteries for you. *(Pause.)*
VIOLET.   I'll come, of course.
SHERLOCK.   I shall look forward to your visit. *(Pause.)* Well. I suppose I must go now.
LADY CARRINGTON.   How do you plan to get home?
SHERLOCK.   The 12: 43 from Victoria. I should just be able to make it.
VIOLET.   The 12: 43 only runs at the week end.
SHERLOCK.   Oh, yes. Of course. *(Pause. Sherlock is trapped. The ladies exchange glances both conspiratorial and quietly gleeful.)*
LADY CARRINGTON.   *(To Sherlock.)* I'm afraid you're out of luck. *(Lady Carrington looks at Violet, who is still relishing the scene.*

Affectionately but firmly.) Good night, my dear. Until tomorrow.

VIOLET.   *('Getting' it.)* Oh. Yes. I see. *(Violet begins to gather her things. Sherlock is just able to look at her.)*

SHERLOCK.   Good night, my dear.

VIOLET.   Good night. *(Violet goes, leaving her parents looking at one another.)*

A NOTE FROM THE AUTHOR

The voice over "dream" moments at the beginning of Act One, Scenes 1 and 2, and Act Two, Scenes 5 and 7, are optional. They can be integrated into the forward movement of the piece, helping to cover scene shifts and act as a kind of "dissolve" — but they should not be allowed to slow down the drive of the action. (If you wish to use them, and to go in the direction of stylization, you may add shadowy figures on stage.)

By early in the second act many (if not all) audience members will have arrived at an opinion about who is Violet's mother. The tension line in the second act is taken over by the blackmail/murder plot, and the "mother mystery" necessarily recedes into the background.

The pronunciation of Turlough O'Brennan's Gaelic phrase "Scathain istigh scathain; doras taobh thall doras" is as follows:

Sca-*how*-an ish-*tee* sca-*how*-an; *dhur*-as *tay*-ev hal *dhur*-as.

Some companies may wish to put the Workman in Act One, Scene 5 in the program, complete with bogus actor's name and bio.

PROPERTY LIST

Papers strewn on table (SHERLOCK)
Tea tray (SHERLOCK) with:
    teacups
    saucers
    cream
    sugar
Tea tray (VIOLET) with:
    teacups
    saucers
    cream
    sugar
    cakes
    toast
Bouquet of flowers (CHARLES)
Silver vase (CHARLES)
Books (VIOLET):
    Adventures of Sherlock Holmes
    The Return of Sherlock Holmes
Tablecloth (TURLOUGH)
Eerie séance objects (TURLOUGH)
Clay model, unfinished (VIOLET)
Clay (VIOLET)
Milliner's bill (VIOLET SMITH)
Slip of paper with address (MRS. MORTON)
Notebook (VIOLET)
Fresh-picked flowers (IRENE)
Blanket (SHERLOCK)
Handkerchief (SHERLOCK)
Note in envelope (CHARLES)
Gun (CHARLES, JACK, VIOLET)
Bullets (CHARLES)
Flashlight (VIOLET)
Handbag (VIOLET)
Birth document (VIOLET)

SOUND EFFECTS

Loud buzzing, as a swarm of bees
Baby crying
Bell ringing
Horn sounding
Piano music
Violin music
Ethereal, mystical music
Creak of a gate
Female voice singing something operatic, classical

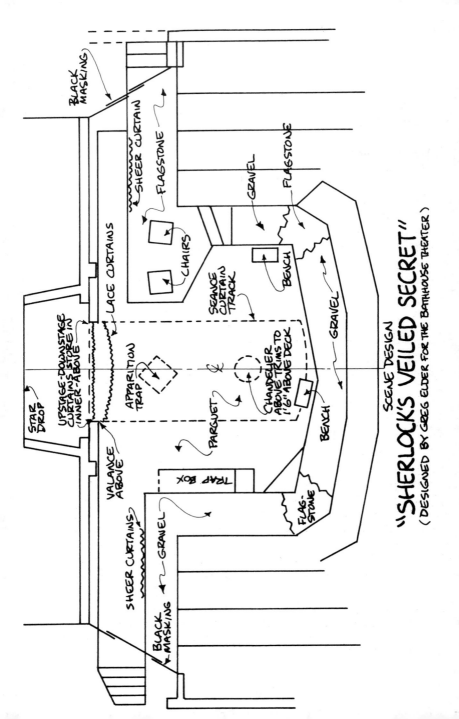

"SHERLOCK'S VEILED SECRET"

(DESIGNED BY GREG ELDER FOR THE BATHHOUSE THEATER)

SCENE DESIGN

NEW
PLAYS

THE AFRICAN COMPANY PRESENTS
RICHARD III
by Carlyle Brown

EDWARD ALBEE'S
FRAGMENTS and THE MARRIAGE PLAY

IMAGINARY LIFE
by Peter Parnell

MIXED EMOTIONS
by Richard Baer

THE SWAN
by Elizabeth Egloff

Write for information as to
availability
DRAMATISTS PLAY SERVICE, Inc.
440 Park Avenue South   New York, N.Y. 10016

NEW
PLAYS

THE LIGHTS
by Howard Korder

THE TRIUMPH OF LOVE
by James Magruder

LATER LIFE
by A.R. Gurney

THE LOMAN FAMILY PICNIC
by Donald Margulies

A PERFECT GANESH
by Terrence McNally

SPAIN
by Romulus Linney

Write for information as to
availability
DRAMATISTS PLAY SERVICE, Inc.
440 Park Avenue South   New York, N.Y. 10016

NEW
PLAYS

LONELY PLANET
by Steven Dietz

THE AMERICA PLAY
by Suzan-Lori Parks

THE FOURTH WALL
by A.R. Gurney

JULIE JOHNSON
by Wendy Hammond

FOUR DOGS AND A BONE
by John Patrick Shanley

DESDEMONA, A PLAY ABOUT A
HANDKERCHIEF
by Paula Vogel

Write for information as to
availability
DRAMATISTS PLAY SERVICE, Inc.
440 Park Avenue South   New York, N.Y. 10016